DER·ZEIT·IHRE·KVNST
DER·KVNST·IHRE·FREIHEIT

1000 PHOTOS of MINERALS and FOSSILS

Text
Alain Eid

Photography
Michel Viard

To Christine Lequin…

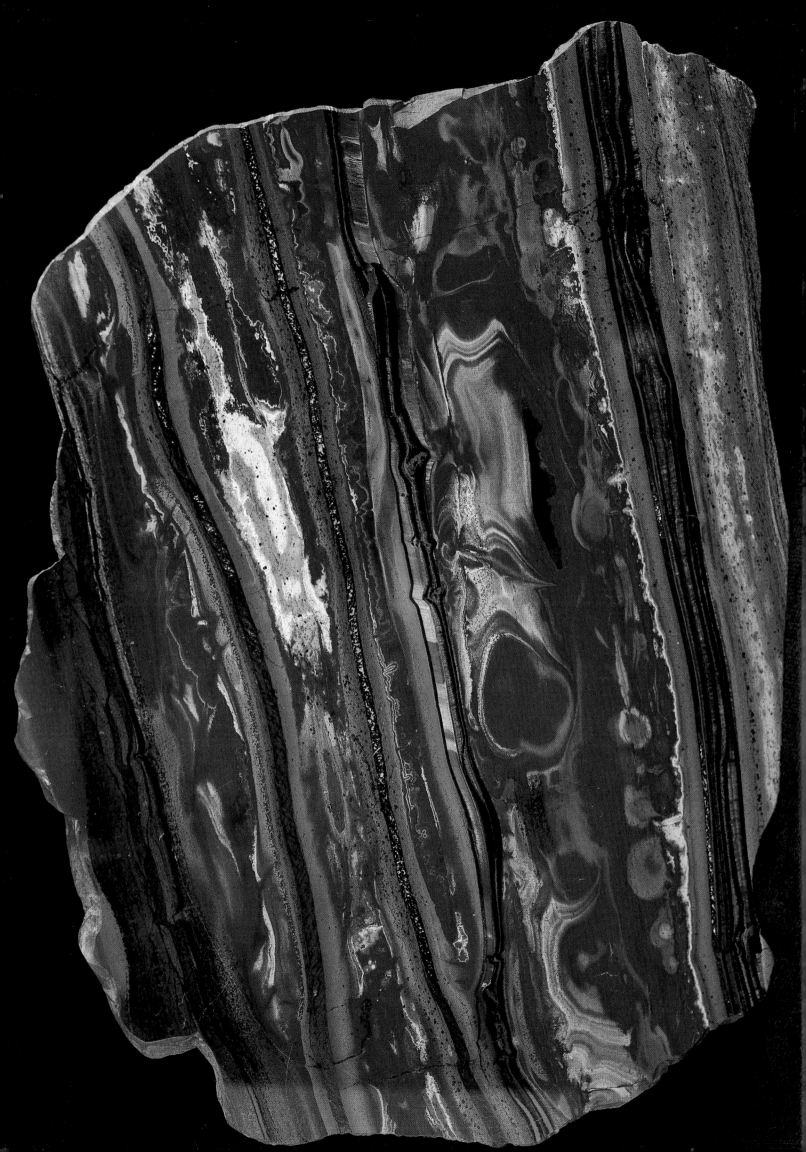

TABLE OF CONTENTS

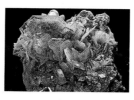

The World
of Gems

A diamond weighing 5.07 carats (1.014 g–0.035 oz.). Diamonds contain only carbon. They are not very different chemically from graphite, which is mined for pencils.

A sapphire weighing 16.51 carats (3.302 g–0.116 oz.). Sapphires, colored blue by iron and titanium, belong to the same family as rubies.

An emerald weighing 2.3 carats (0.4 g–0.014 oz.). Imperceptible traces of chromium oxide give the emerald its deep green color. Emeralds belong to the beryl family of minerals.

A ruby weighing 5 carats (1 g–0.035 oz.). Rubies are corundum, a compound of oxygen and aluminum colored red by a tiny quantity of chromium.

Precious Stones

Only diamonds, rubies, sapphires, and emeralds can rightly be called precious stones. These are the most beautiful, the rarest, and the most expensive stones used in jewelry. In South Africa, at least 18 tons of ore must be removed from underground to obtain 1 g (0.035 oz.) of diamond. The mined crystal is dull and grayish; after all, it is only carbon. Pure crystallized carbon, yes, a "supercarbon" perhaps, but it has to go under the lapidary's wheel to show its brilliance. Removed from the rough, polished, and cut, a good 3-carat (0.6 g) specimen may be worth up to $100,000. Rubies and sapphires are rather ordinary compounds of oxygen and aluminum that belong to the corundum family. Several chromium atoms are incorporated into this formula to give rubies their incandescent red color, and this makes all the difference. Pigeon's-blood rubies, one of the rarest varieties, are found only in the Mogok Valley in Burma, and can easily equal diamonds in value. Sapphires, colored blue by iron and titanium, are not as rare; crystals weighing several tens of carats are not exceptional. But a beautiful specimen from Sri Lanka can be worth $6,000 per carat. Emeralds are the rarest of the precious stones; in Colombia, the chances of finding one in the surrounding ore are about one in 90 million. On a weight basis, emeralds cost four times the price of diamonds. Globally, these four precious stones represent 97 percent of the value of gems in circulation in the world.

An emerald weighing 14.86 carats (3 g–0.105 oz.), worth $300,000. Emeralds, the softest precious stones, are four times the price of diamonds.

Raw emerald on calcite encrusted with pyrite. Colombia is the major world producer of emeralds. The Muzo mines were already exploited during the time of the Incas.

Raw emeralds from Brazil. The largest emerald ever discovered was found in Colombia in 1961. It weighed almost 1.5 kg (3.3 lb.) in gross weight.

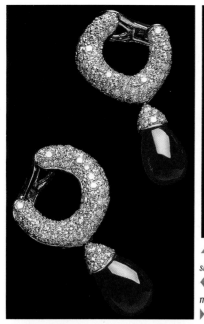

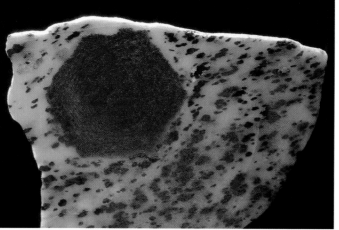

▲ *Ruby in zoisite. Encased in zoisite, this ruby cannot be used as a gem. Cut into thin slabs and polished, it can be used as a decorative object.*

◀ *Rubies mounted as pendants on earrings. Pigeon's-blood rubies, the most precious, are mined in the Mogok Valley, in Burma.*

▶ *Statuette in ruby and zoisite carved from a block found in Tanzania.*

The Cullinan

The largest diamond ever found was the Cullinan, discovered in 1905 in South Africa. Its raw weight was 3.106 carats (621 g–21.74 oz./1 lb. 5.74 oz.). It was broken up into about 100 gems, one of which, the Star of Africa, weighs 530.20 carats (106 g–3.71 oz.), the largest cut diamond in the world to date. All the stones taken from the Cullinan belong to the crown of England.

◀ *A 6.40-carat diamond (1.28 g–0.045 oz.) mounted in a ring can cost as much as $300,000. South Africa is currently the primary producer of gem diamonds.*

▼ *Diamonds mounted in jewelry (valued at $350,000). About 18 tons of ore must be treated to obtain 1 g (0.035 oz.) of diamond.*

▶ *The Ruspoli, a sapphire weighing 135.8 carats (27 g– 0.945 oz.), was the property of Louis XIV. This cube-shaped cut is no longer done today.*

▼ *A sapphire weighing 4.09 carats (0.81 g–0.028 oz.) mounted as a ring. Its name, taken from the old Hebrew word sappir, means "the marvel of the world."*

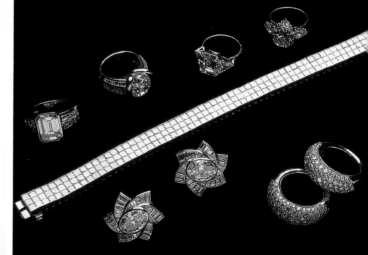

◀ ▶ *Sapphires encased in rock. Most corundum cannot be used as gems; however, they can be used in industry, especially as abrasives.*

▶ *For 2,500 years, sapphires have been mined in the Ratnapura region of Sri Lanka, up until the last century, the only known source of sapphires.*

▲ *Sapphire prospectors in Sri Lanka. Using long wooden poles, they drag the river gravel in search of the precious crystal.*

▲ *In Sri Lanka, one-third of sapphire production is done this way, in river gravel.*

▼ *About 30,000 Sri Lankan prospectors use screens along the banks of rivers every day looking for sapphires.*

Sapphire Mining

Until the last century, the Ratnapura region in present-day Sri Lanka was the only known source of sapphires. In Singhalese, Ratnapura means "city of gems" because this area also abounds in rubies, zircon, topaz, and garnet. Every day, 30,000 prospectors infected by "blue fever" scour this territory, barely 100 km (62 mi.) long. Gathered along river banks, they scratch the alluvial gravel with long poles. The sapphires lie at the bottom, having been eroded from their source rock millions of years ago, then transported here by the current. Others seek sapphires directly at the source, that is, underground. With shovels, they dig narrow passages to reach the closest pockets of sapphires, located many feet under the surface. The quantities brought to the surface are small, but the discovery of a sapphire weighing more than 20 carats (4 g–0.14 oz.) is not unheard of, the record being a raw crystal weighing 20 kg (44 lb.). The prospectors' work is regulated by the State Gem Corporation, which issues mining licenses and is in charge of selling the stones to foreign countries—theoretically at least, because smuggling is common. Cambodia and Thailand have become significant producers of the blue stones in this century, along with Burma, the United States, and Australia, to a lesser degree, but sapphires from Sri Lanka are still the most abundant, representing half the world's production.

▲ *Raw sapphire.*

▲ *Sapphires can also be mined from underground. Here, the entrance to a mine in the Ratnapura region, whose name means "city of gems."*

◀ *In spite of the discovery of deposits in Cambodia, Burma, and Thailand, Sri Lanka still supplies half the world's production of sapphires.*

▲ *Brought to the surface, the rubble is filtered through a screen. The heaviest stones remain at the bottom, along with a precious sapphire perhaps.*

▲ *Using traditional methods, miners descend almost 100 m (328 ft.) in depth. It often takes several weeks to discover a pocket of sapphires.*

▲ *The rough stones brought from the mines are carefully examined by local buyers, in sunlight or using electric lights.*

▲ *The stones brought up from the galleries are sorted mechanically; sapphires usually occur in rough crystals weighing several pounds.*
▼ *A second sorting is done by hand to collect the smallest crystals.*

▲ *Rough sapphires from the mines are sent to Beruwala, a city located 100 km (62 mi.) from Colombo, where they are cut.*

▼ *The cut stone market in Beruwala. Every day merchants come from Colombo, the capital of Sri Lanka.*

◀ *The most important sapphire mines in the world are located in Kanchanaburi, Thailand. The deposits are uncovered by bulldozer. Sapphires from Thailand are in less demand than those of Sri Lanka, not being as transparent or blue.*

▼ *Sapphire deposits were discovered in Thailand in 1870, but they were not mined until the twentieth century.*

▼ *Sapphire cutting in the province of Kanchanaburi. In Thailand, one million people support themselves by cutting sapphires in their homes.*

▲ *Sapphires are first attached to small brass sticks, then polished on a grinding wheel and faceted.*

▲ *The examination of a sapphire with a jeweler's loupe. The quality of a sapphire is best seen in the twilight when its brilliance is at its most subtle.*

▶ *Sapphire cabochon. Because sapphire crystals are often enormous (10 carats, or 2 g, or 0.07 oz. are not rare), they lend themselves well to being cut into cabochons.*

▲ *About 95 percent of the sapphires sold on the Asian market have been heated to more than 1,700°C (3,092°F) to color them blue, at the risk of breaking them.*

▼ *Only the blue varieties of corundum are called sapphires in the jewelry trade. The others are called green sapphires, yellow sapphires, and so on.*

▼ *Many sapphires sold in Thailand, are, in fact, smuggled from Burma or from Cambodia.*

A Sapphire Industry

A sapphire is an aluminum oxide that contains minute quantities of iron and titanium to color it blue. Everything is a question of proportion, because the iron content can also color the stone yellow, green, mauve, violet, or orange. But only the blue varieties can carry the name sapphire in jewelry; the others must be called yellow sapphires, green sapphires, mauve sapphires, and so on. Much more abundant underground, they never equal the price of the blue sapphires. To give them extra value, Asian lapidaries usually turn them blue artificially by heating. This operation requires a great deal of dexterity; the rough crystal is put into the oven at temperatures ranging from 1,700°C (3,092°F) to 1,900°C (3,452°F), protected by a ceramic pot that prevents the stone from breaking when it is in contact with the fire. Almost all the sapphires produced in Thailand or Sri Lanka are "enhanced" in this way, not actually involving any deception, just giving nature a hand. In this way, the blue stone avoids being extremely rare. Fortunately for the stone lover, its average cost does not exceed $1,500 per carat (0.2 g–0.007 oz.). This being so, an unheated specimen with exceptional clarity is still rare, like a diamond, ruby, or emerald. A French blue sapphire, an exceptional variety from Sri Lanka, is worth up to ten times more on the market. It is used only in very expensive jewelry.

▲ *Mauboussin, one of the great Parisian jewelers, uses sapphires from Sri Lanka. The most prized variety is the French blue.*

◀ *Bangkok is the sapphire capital, the center of international commerce. Even sapphires found in the United States or Australia are brought here to be cut.*

▲ The Star of Lanka, a star sapphire weighing 362 carats (72 g–2.52 oz.) is a national treasure of Sri Lanka. It is exhibited behind an armored display and guarded by a cobra.

▲ Most of the jewelry workshops in Thailand are located in Bangkok, the capital.

▶ In Thailand, western buyers of cut stones deal with large merchants in Bangkok, who are often Chinese.

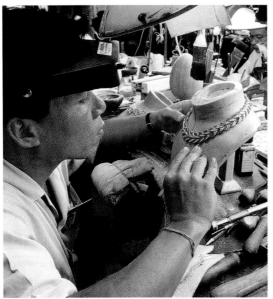

▲ A jewelry workshop in Bangkok, Thailand.

▼ Sapphires with artificially enhanced blue color average $1,500 per carat (0.2 g–0.007 oz.).

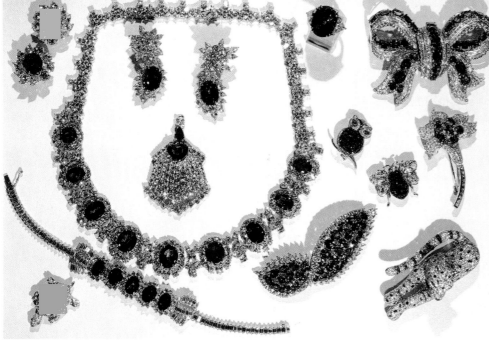

▲ Selection of sapphire and diamond jewelry made in Thailand.

▲ *Aquamarine can occur as giant crystals. An incredible crystal weighing 110 kg (242 lb.) was discovered in Brazil, the largest supplier of this gem.*

Fine Stones

Out of the 3,500 species of minerals in the world, barely 100 are classified as gemstones. A gemstone is any specimen that can be cut and mounted in jewelry. To be faceted, a stone must possess the precious optical quality of transparency, together with sufficient hardness (a minimum of 7, the hardness of quartz), to avoid breaking on the lapidary's wheel.

Because diamonds, rubies, sapphires, and emeralds possess these qualities of transparency and hardness to the highest degree, they are designated as precious stones. The others are called fine stones, the term "semi-precious" now being outlawed in jewelry.

Among fine stones, transparency is not required; stones tend to be translucent, which allows light to reflect within the crystal much less successfully. Rarity is another quality of gems, and it is indispensable, since this is what determines the stone's cost. It makes all the difference between a precious variety and a fine variety. The aquamarine belongs to the same family as the emerald, but the fact that it is mined in crystals weighing several pounds gives it a much lower value on the market. In certain cases, rarity and price can act in favor of a fine stone.

Benitoite is an extremely rare stone with beautiful clear crystals, known to occur in only one deposit in California. When it is faceted, it exceeds the per carat price of a sapphire.

▲ *Its blue-green color gave aquamarine its name, meaning "seawater." Aquamarine is found underground and in riverbeds.*

▶ *Long ago, clear beryl crystals (seen here, morganite) were used to make eyeglasses, at one time called beryls.*

▲ *Morganite, lilac pink in color, is the most abundant of the beryl gems. The most beautiful crystals come from Madagascar or Brazil.*

▲ *Blue beryl. While emerald, aquamarine, heliodor, and morganite are the rarest beryls, others are significant source rocks for beryllium, a metal.*

▼ *Tigereye, crocidolite that is partially replaced by quartz, is valued for its tawny tones, but is impossible to facet.*

▲ Chrysoberyl (shown here, a rough crystal) is mined in the rivers of Sri Lanka, where it is associated with sapphire prospecting.

▶ Chrysoberyl: etymologically "golden beryl," although from a different family. Hardest gem (8.5) after diamonds (10) and corundum (9).

◀ Kyanite (or disthene) on quartz. Its blue crystals are often 30 cm (12 in.) in length and, rarely transparent; thus, they are often cut into cabochons.

◀ The golden yellow color of this beryl gave it the Greek name of heliodor, "gift of the sun." It is of radioactive origin.

▼ Sphene (titanite). Faceted as the brilliant cut, sphene has a brilliance comparable to diamonds. Unfortunately it is rare to find it in clear crystal form.

Rediscovered Olivine

Gem quality olivine, or peridot, comes primarily from the island of Zebirget (or Saint John) in the Red Sea. This deposit was already mined by the Egyptians 3,500 years ago. Kept secret for centuries in order not to attract greedy pirates who, it was feared, would steal it, it was completely forgotten until 1900, when it was rediscovered.

▼ Feldspars make up more than half of the minerals in the earth's crust. The iridescent varieties (shown here, amazonites) are the most sought after.

▼ Amazonite. Its name comes from the Amazon River of Brazil, where it is mined along with jade. Cut as a cabochon, it is often confused with jade.

▲ Aventurines, sunstone variety. This reddish orange feldspar owes its fiery reflections to fine inclusions of hematite in the crystal.

▲ Labradorites. Discovered in Labrador, this feldspar is valued as a decorative stone for its iridescent reflections.

▶ Indicolite tourmaline. This blue variety of tourmaline is highly valued, but it is necessary to heat it to clarify the crystal.

▶ Watermelon tourmaline. A two-colored variety, the crystal is green tinged with red at its center.

◀ Many tourmalines are not suitable for faceting, because inclusions often cause them to be dark. Pink rubellite is the clearest, and is thus the most often faceted.

The Art of Gem Cutting

A rough crystal, even a precious stone, has no more appeal than a stone; it requires all the lapidary's skill to give it the shape that will reflect light with maximum intensity. In this process, the crystal will lose more than half its volume. It will be broken up bit by bit, sawed, and polished, in order to obtain the rounded shape necessary for the application of facets. Each gem requires a certain type of cut depending on its shape and optical properties. The round brilliant cut with 56 facets is commonly used in jewelry; it is traditionally used on diamonds and all stones that have a high index of refraction. The step cut, square or rectangular, is used for gems with little surface brilliance. The effect of light is obtained by faceting the stone on its sides and in the angles. This cut requires large crystals, at a minimum of 4 carats in the case of emerald, which gives its name to this cut. The pear cut is a variation of the round brilliant cut, pointed at one end; it is used for stones that are mounted as pendants on earrings, from which it gets its name of pendant. The marquise or needle cut is obviously a more elongated shape, pointed at both ends; the baguette is rectangular.

The lapidary's creativity is actually unlimited, and can result in imaginative cuts, such as triangles, roses, hearts, and others.

▲ Rubellite tourmaline. This tourmaline was brought from Ceylon by Dutch sailors at the beginning of the eighteenth century. Its prism-shaped crystals are characteristic.

▲ Grossularite garnet. The pink grossularite from Mexico is in less demand than its cousin from Kenya, the emerald green tsavarite, which was discovered in 1967.
◀ Andradite garnet. Brown, black, or yellow, the andra-dite also occurs as a rarer form, the green demantoid, which comes from the Ural Mountains.

▲ Garnet is one of the oldest cut stones. Specimens more than 5,000 years old have been found in a tomb in Czechnia, pierced for stringing as a necklace.
◀ Almandine garnet. Known since the Middle Ages under the name of carbuncle ("little carbon"), the almandine was as a talis-man during the Crusades.

The Brazil Beauty

The orangey-yellow imperial topaz is the most precious of topazes. It comes primarily from Minas Gerais in Brazil. Faceted, its crystal has the brilliance of a diamond. It took some time for experts to determine that the famous Braganza diamond weighing 1,680 carats (336 g–11.76 oz.), owned by Portugal, was actually a topaz.

▼ Spodumene, kunzite variety. This pink variety of spodumene, more common than hiddenite, was discovered in California in 1903.

◀ Blue topaz (rough crystal weighing 2 kg–4.4 lb.). When heated, topazes often change color. Only the blue variety, called "safira," is unchangeable.

▶ Hiddenite spodumene. Spodumene rarely occurs in crystals suitable for faceting. The chrome green hiddenite is an exception.

◀ Violet fluorite on calcite. The Chinese carve delicate teapots out of fluorine, with great patience, because the stone has a hardness of 4 and is difficult to work with.

▲ Brown fluorine with sphalerite crystals. Transparent fluorite can be faceted but it has a tendency to discolor with time.

▲ Zircon, hyacinth variety. The most highly prized zircons are mined from the rivers of Sri Lanka. When they are cut, their brilliance resembles that of diamond and they are often sold as such.

◀ Pink smithsonite on pyrrhotite. Smithsonite is not hard enough to cut. This variety has a purely decorative value.

▲ Blue smithsonite (from the former collection of Paquebot France). Cut into cabochons, blue smithsonite can resemble turquoise.

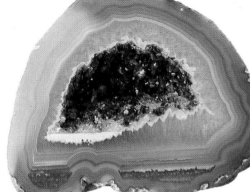

▲ *Smoky quartz.*

Quartz Gems

Q uartz is a variety of crystallized silica, a relative of the opal (which never occurs as crystals). It is one of the most abundant minerals in nature. It can be found in crystals weighing several tons as well as in a microscopic form in the desert sand. By itself, it makes up 12 percent of the earth's crust. Indispensable for the manufacturing of glass since ancient times, it is also prized as a gem because its hardness is ideal (7) and its transparency is exemplary. Its large-sized crystals make it ideal for working into cabochons. But a beautiful clear quartz also lends itself to a brilliant cut, sparkling on its 56 facets similar to a diamond. Quartz is naturally colorless; it is a rock crystal (or hyaline quartz). When foreign bodies are incorporated into its crystal, superb colored varieties are produced, which are highly sought after for jewelry. Thus, traces of manganese give rise to rose quartz; small inclusions of crocidolite produce blue quartz (sapphire quartz); inclusions of mica create green quartz (aventurine quartz). Amethyst is colored violet by the addition of iron. The dark varieties generally have more value than light varieties, because the stone has an unfortunate tendency to discolor when exposed to light. A small addition of iron can also color the quartz yellow, this time producing citrine, a gem that resembles topaz. Because it is rather rare underground, the majority of specimens available on the market are actually amethysts, colored yellow by heating to more than 500°C (932°F).

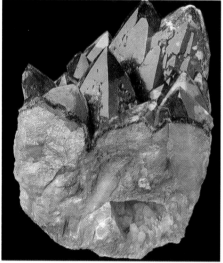

▲ *Heated with a flame, smoky quartz can turn yellow, producing a citrine.*

▼ *Smoky quartz that is totally black is called morion quartz. It is much in demand because it is transparent.*

▲ *Quartz is a mineral that is very abundant in nature. Its hardness is (7). Because of its transparency, it is ideal for cutting.*

▲ *Radiating milky quartz. This is a variety of quartz that is completely white.*

▲ *Citrines. Naturally yellow quartz, or citrine quartz, is rare. The majority of those sold on the market are amethysts heated to 500°C (932°F).*

◀ *Colorless quartz is rock crystal quartz. Ancient people thought that it was water frozen so hard that fire could not make it melt.*

▶ *Crystallized rose quartz is especially rare, as opposed to solid varieties. It comes from Brazil and Madagascar.*

▲ *Hematoid quartz, so called because of its blood-red color.*
▼ *A natural radioactive source can color the rock crystal brown, thus producing smoky or smoked quartz.*

▲ *Quartz, aventurine variety. Fine inclusions of mica make the quartz green. Very prized in China, it is associated with jade under the name "imperial Yu stone."*

▲ *Smoky quartz with well-defined crystals. The most valuable smoky quartz comes from Saint-Gothard, Switzerland. Some crystals reach 130 kg (286 lb.).*

▲ *Rose quartz, the rarest of the colored quartz. The pink color is due to the presence of an infinitesimal amount of manganese in the crystal.*

The Bacchus Stone

According to legend, Bacchus was attracted to one of the nymphs of the goddess Diana. To protect her from his passion, Diana transformed her into a pure rock crystal. The god felt such resentment that he poured his cup of wine over the stone, thus creating amethyst. Not so farfetched— amethyst is a rock crystal colored violet by iron.

▶ *Here, a dogtooth amethyst, which is so called because of its partially colored crystals that resemble teeth.*

◀ *Fragment of an amethyst geode. Because of its rarity, amethyst was for a long time considered a precious stone in Europe.*

▲ *Chalcedony, carnelian variety. Red carnelian was formerly used to make royal seals. It has always been worked in Tibet.*

▶ *Agate. Its name is from the Achate River in Sicily, where it was discovered. The deposits have now been exhausted.*

▲ *Snakeskin chalcedony. Chalcedony is poorly crystallized quartz, abundant in sedimentary rocks. When it is translucent, it is suitable for cutting.*

Chalcedony, Agate, and Jasper

Quartz does not always occur as separate crystals. Chalcedony crystals are so small, so intermingled within each other that a microscope is necessary to distinguish them. The texture of chalcedony is such that it is never transparent, but translucent, so it cannot be faceted. The Greeks and Romans used to carve it to make glasses or to engrave it in relief to make cameos; it has the hardness of quartz.

Chrysoprase is a chalcedony with a minute amount of nickel to color it green, which makes it resemble jade. Carnelian is colored red by hematite. Sard, a more brownish red, was named for the area where it was mined—Sardinia, a deposit exhausted long ago. Agates are a particular type of chalcedony.

Formed around a nucleus of silica or other foreign body, they are deposited in fine concentric layers of various colors; alternating white and black is characteristic of onyx, for example.

Agates are traditionally named for the scenes they depict: moss agate, feather agate, star agate. The motifs are emphasized when the stone is cut into a polished slab or shaped into balls. Jasper is a rock made up of more than 80 percent micro-crystalline quartz. Opal and chalcedony are also present. Impurities give rise to the colors (green, red, or brown) and the irregular arrangement of the motifs, either in bands or in spots. Although this impure silica is not translucent, it can be used to carve decorative objects, as with chalcedony.

▲ *Rose agate. Agate is chalcedony, which is deposited in fine concentric layers of different colors around a foreign body.*

▼ *Moss agate. The agate name is often related to the scene agate depicts: moss, feather, and so on.*

▲ *Chalcedony, chrysoprase variety. Green chrysoprase is the most valued variety of chalcedony. It is also called jade in Australia, because of the significant deposits in that country.*

▶ *Plume agate. It has been in demand since the time of the Babylonians who used it for making jewelry or drinking cups.*

▲ Onyx is a two-colored agate with black and white layers. Its name comes from the Latin onyx, "fingernail," because it is as transparent as one.

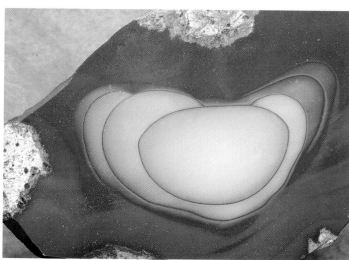

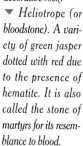

◀ Brown jasper. Contrary to chalcedony, jasper is opaque and therefore it cannot be cut. It is considered primarily a decorative rock.

▼ Heliotrope (or bloodstone). A variety of green jasper dotted with red due to the presence of hematite. It is also called the stone of martyrs for its resemblance to blood.

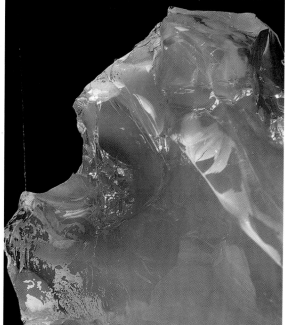

▲ Kalahari jasper. Jasper is a siliceous rock, which is made up primarily of finely granular quartz. Jasper also contains chalcedony and opal.

▶ Red jasper. The presence of iron in the rock, along with other impurities, give it the red color.

Precious Opal

Opal is a mineral closely related to quartz, made up of 80 percent silica, but not in the form of a crystal. Only transparent varieties are sought after for faceting, especially the fire opal (below) with orange-red reflections. Its reputation as a jinx dates from the last century, but for a long time previously it was considered a protective stone. In the jewelry business, it is given the enviable title of the fifth precious stone.

▶ The state of Rio Grande do Sul, in Brazil, provides the most beautiful agates available on the market today.

▼ Jasper from South Africa, one of the main suppliers of jasper; the rock was already known by the Greeks and Romans, who carved it.

▲ Bull's-eye. Quartz with inclusions of crocidolite is colored in bands like jasper.

▼ Orbicular jasper. The jasper varieties that have spots or chains are called by descriptive names such as orbicular, flowered, or porcelain jasper.

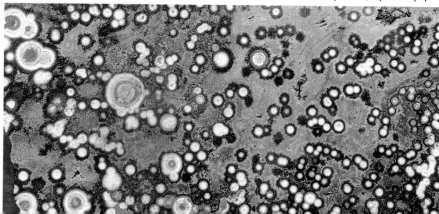

▲ *Lapis lazuli necklace. Its name, taken from medieval Latin, means "azure stone." It is a decorative blue rock made up of mostly lazurite.*

▶ *Sodalite. This mineral is often used to imitate lapis lazuli, but it is more violet than lapis lazuli and much more abundant.*

▲ *Lazulite. Its bright blue color causes it to be confused with lazurite or sodalite, but it is rare as crystals and should not be confused with azurite.*

▲ *Chrysocolla is an amorphous mineral that is impossible to cut. It is found in the famous "Elat stone," the symbol of Israel.*

▶ *Charoite is a mineral that is very prized for decoration; it was discovered along the Chara River, in Siberia, from which it gets its name.*

▲ *Marcasite dollar. Marcasite naturally forms strange concretions called dollars, used as decoration.*

Ornamental Stones

A mineral may have all the esthetic qualities of color and fire, but if it lacks transparency, or if its hardness is too low, it is by definition unsuitable for cutting. Since it is possible to carve it or to polish it into a cabochon, it is considered an ornamental or decorative stone in the jewelry business. Some rocks such as jet, a brilliant black lignite, obsidian, a volcanic glass, or even lapis lazuli are in this category. Lapis lazuli owes its color to the presence of a blue mineral, lazurite, mixed with sodalite, diopside, mica, and pyrite. It was already very actively traded in Mesopotamia, more than 5,000 years ago; it went into making royal seals and sacred statues. From there, the rock was exported to Egypt where it was used for decoration on the tombs of the pharoahs. In seeking to imitate its colors, Egyptian ceramists succeeded in inventing enamel. The only lapis lazuli deposit known in ancient times was that of the Sar-e-Sang mine, in present-day Afghanistan. It is still active and continues to provide the most beautiful lapis lazuli in the world. The vein, however, shows signs of being exhausted; with an annual production of barely 1 ton, the rock is rather costly on the market.

Deposits have been discovered more recently in Chile, Iran, and California but the quality is not there; with too much sodalite and not enough lazurite, the "azure stone" changes to a more violet color over time.

▲ *Lapis lazuli Buddha.*

▲ *Opaque, turquoise does not lend itself to faceting, but it has always been used as a stone to be carved; the Chinese made opium containers out of it.*

◀ *Azurite. This blue mineral, known since ancient times, is too soft to be faceted but it can be worked into cabochons.*

▶ Rhodochrosite was formerly used by the South American Indians to make statuettes. For this reason, it is sometimes called the Inca rose.

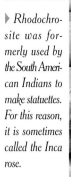

▼ Mammelar rhodochrosite. Very breakable, rhodochrosite (or dialogite) cannot be faceted, but it can be polished or carved.

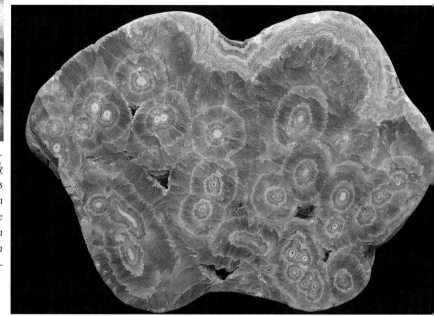

◀ Banded obsidian. Obsidian is a glassy rock that is rich in silica. It is of volcanic origin. When it is transparent, it can be faceted, but it is most often opaque. Banded obsidian is used for making precious decorative objects.

◀ Speckled obsidian. Obsidian casts silvery reflections in the light. Rainbows made up of red, green, or gold bands are the most in demand.

▼ Hematite (or oligiste). Its shadowy red ranging to black has long led to this decorative rock being used for making jewelry for mourners.

◀ Left, top, an Aztec head in obsidian. Like flint, obsidian breaks into sharp-edged blades. Indians made arrowheads from it or carved it.

◀ Left, bottom, Mamellar malachite. Malachite is traditionally worked into cabochons. It can also be carved to make vases or cameos.

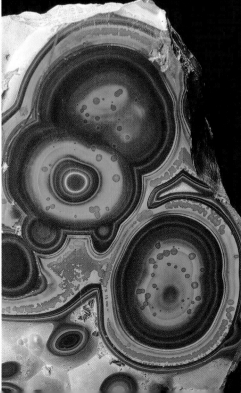

Immortal Jade

The term jade is used to refer to two distinct minerals: nephrite (on the left), and jadeite. Both of these types of jade are opaque and never occur as crystals. Jade is worked into cabochons or carved to make decorative objects. For at least 4,000 years, the Chinese have worked jade and consider it to be an immortal stone.

Frauds and Imitations

▲ *Buddha in aventurine glass. A simple colored glass imitates sunstone aventurine perfectly.*

▼ *Sunstone aventurine. Because it is particularly sought after for its fiery reflections, it is rather rare in nature and is often imitated.*

Without profound knowledge of gemology, the amateur risks being fooled by the sparkle of a stone. And it can be an expensive mistake—remember, all that glitters is not gold. The verb "glitter" was taken from the word "beryl" in the Middle Ages; it means to "be like a beryl," an ordinary stone that was once considered precious only because of its sparkle. This is also the case with zircon or topaz, which can easily be mistaken for diamond when cut into 56 facets. An unscrupulous seller will give them names like "Madura diamond" (zircon) or "Saxe diamond" (topaz), tricky names that are forbidden by law. Cut glass imitation of transparent gems was already practiced by Egyptian lapidaries around 1600 B.C. This is the source of all the "doublets" for which unsuspecting consumers pay dearly every day—jewels with the table facet of diamonds, but the base is ordinary glass.

Coloring is another classic in the art of "finishing" a stone. It can also be attributed to Egyptian producers of fake stones, who 7,000 years ago were using colored earthenware to imitate turquoise. Today, lapis lazuli of "pure Afghan extraction" may well be colored marble made very near your own home. The same is true for jade and many amethysts from Brazil. A stone covered with a plastic coloring material is less likely to scratch under a fingernail; many emeralds from Colombia sold on the black market in the streets of Bogota are nothing but plasticized quartz.

Heating is a more subtle technique that enhances the color of a stone as it is heated in an oven. At 350°C (662°F), a yellow topaz becomes red; at 500°C (932°F) an amethyst changes into yellow quartz. Their value is multiplied and the amateur sees only the fire. Here the trickery is relative, because the process is completely natural; everything is made evident by the color.

▲ *The technique of cutting glass to imitate gems, practiced by the Egyptians, is still practiced today. Shown here, a glass necklace that imitates amethyst.*

◀▲ *Agates colored blue and red with mineral dyes. Seven thousand years ago, Egyptian ceramists were using colored earthenware to imitate turquoise and lapis lazuli.*

◀ *This smoky quartz is artificially obtained by radiation, but it is devoid of all radioactivity.*

▶ *Amethyst heated to 500°C (932°F) turns into yellow quartz, or citrine. The majority of citrines available on the market are heated amethysts.*

◀ A pricey amethyst should be a beautiful sustained violet color. Imperfectly colored specimens are often dyed, as this specimen, to enhance their value.

▼ A transparent topaz (shown here) can easily imitate a diamond. The misleading name "Saxe diamond" has been forbidden by law.

▲ Zircon (shown here, a raw crystal) can imitate a diamond under the misleading name of "Madura diamond."

▶ All that glitters is not gold. This group of stones from Brazil is very common, and has a low market value in spite of its bright colors and sparkle. The amateur must be careful in choosing.

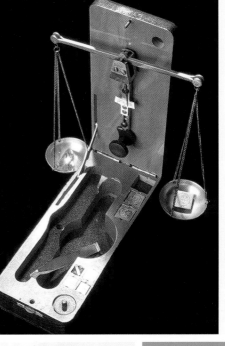

Carob and Carat

The unit of weight for gems is the carat, which is equal to 0.2 g (0.007 oz). The word comes from the Arabic kharruba, carob, a fruit whose seeds have a constant weight of 0.2 g (0.007 oz.); thus, in the Orient, they were used to weigh precious stones. Do not confuse this carat with the gold karat, which is an indication of purity (24 karats for pure gold).

◀ These turquoises have been "stabilized" with a resin that covers them. These are powdery varieties that would otherwise be unsuitable for jewelry.

▶ When faceted, a transparent zircon sparkles with all the fire of a diamond. It can fool an inexperienced eye.

▼ When heated, amethyst can also become green. It then becomes a highly appreciated gem used in making jewelry called prasolite.

▲ Ivory, a gem of organic origin, can be imitated, as here, by a palm seed, but the imitation has an admirable goal: to protect the elephant, the walrus, and the hippopotamus.

▲ Smoky quartz found underground has been exposed to a naturally radioactive source, which has colored it brown.

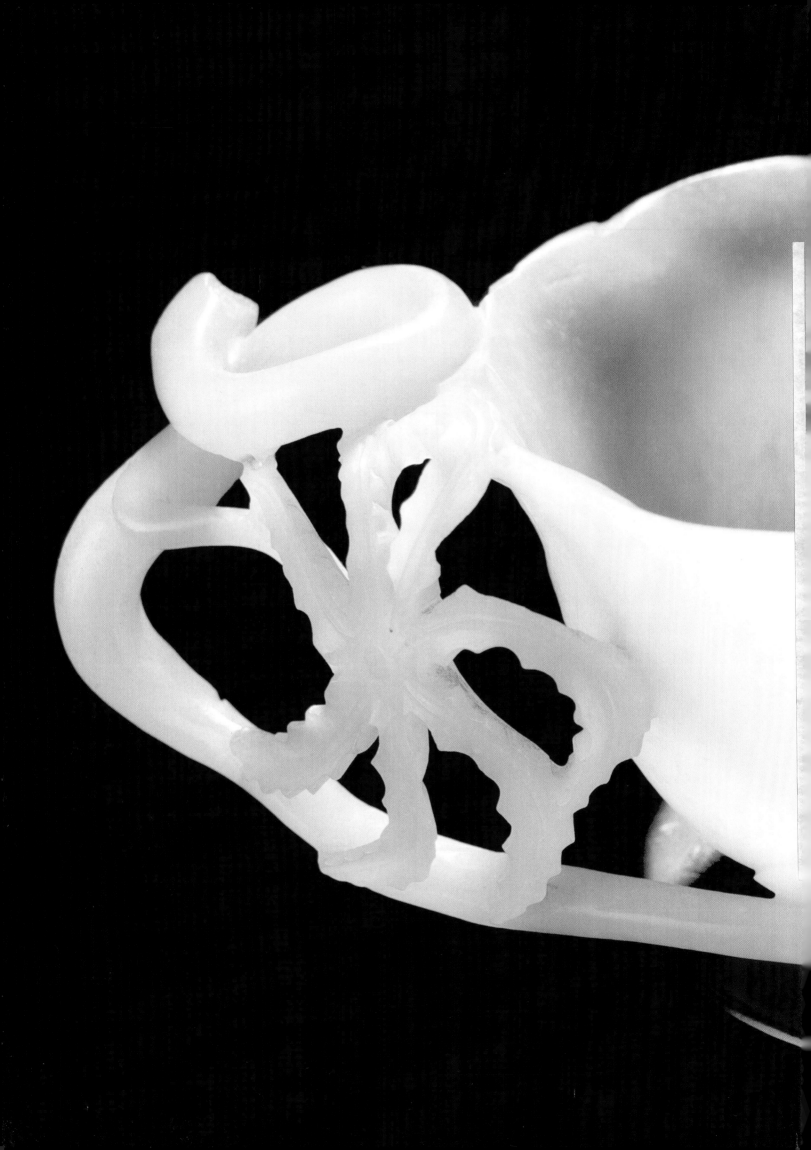

Artistic
Materials

Gold and Precious Metals

Gold nugget.
Alluvial gold occurs as nuggets in rivers. The largest nugget ever found weighed 193 kg (425 lb.) in gross weight.

▼ *Native gold on quartz. Every year 1,450 tons of gold are mined. The most important mining area is in Witwartersrand, South Africa.*

The amount of gold mined by man since the beginning of time is about 80,000 tons. Because this yellow metal is practically unalterable, most of this gold is still in circulation in one form or another because of being remelted. This property, together with its rarity and its perfect malleability, have caused it to be the goldsmith's metal for at least the last 5,000 years. It is found in its native state underground, encrusted in quartz veins or associated with sulfides (pyrite, arsenopyrite), and in riverbeds, where it is deposited because of its high density (19.3) after having been removed from its source rock by the action of wind and water. Silver in its pure state is much more rare than gold, but in nature it forms about 50 compounds, of which the most important for mining are the "red" silvers (proustite, pyrargarite) and the "black" silvers (stephanite, polybasite). With production of 200 tons per year, platinum is the rarest of the precious metals. It was discovered by the Spanish in Colombia in the eighteenth century. Believing it to be a variety of silver, they tried to melt it, but its fusion point of 1,772°C (3,222°F) was much higher than the technology of that time permitted. Refusing to mine it, they gave it the derisive name of platina ("little silver"). Its melting was not accomplished until the next century. Platinum has opened up a large field of applications, as in jewelry where platinum is traditionally used to set precious stones.

▶ *Arsenopyrite, the principal ore mineral associated with gold, gold-bearing quartz, and pyrite, are only mined when there is at least 6 g (0.21 oz.) of gold per ton of ore.*

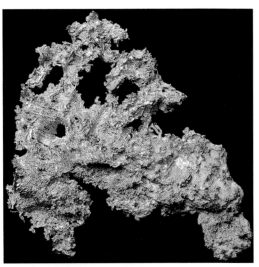

▶ *Gold crystallized as leaves. Native gold rarely occurs as well-formed crystals because its growth is usually constrained by the surrounding rock.*
◀ *Gold leaf. Vein gold is more abundant than gold in water. Caught within the cavities of rocks, it has a curious flattened shape. Very rare in nature, the average concentration of gold in rock is usually only 4 mg (0.00014 oz.) per ton.*

◀ *Gold prospector washing river sand with his pan, the traditional tool of prospectors.*
▼ *Two prospectors straining alluvium. Since ancient times, sheepskin has been used to strain the sand, thus the origin of the Golden Fleece.*

▲ *Extracted from gold-bearing ore (shown here, pyrite), gold occurs as minute flecks, invisible to the naked eye.*

▼ *In riverbeds, the yellow metal can occur as an amalgam, a natural mixture of mercury and gold.*

▼ *Once the mercury is gone, the perfectly pure liquid gold can be recovered from the bottom of the crucible.*

▲ *In order to recover the gold, the amalgam must be heated to make the mercury disappear.*

◀ *Nuggets found in France. In water, gold is mined when it is present in a concentration of only 0.5 g (0.018 oz.) of gold per cu. m (35 cu. ft.) of rock.*

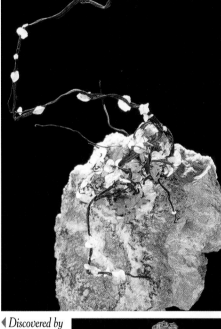

Monetary Metal

Silver has coexisted with gold as a monetary metal for a long time. The first coins were pounded 2,700 years ago in Greece. They were made of electrum, a natural alloy of gold and silver, obtained from straining river sand. It was in what today is known as the Sarabat River (Turkey) that King Croesus mined his legendary fortune.

▶ *Pure silver rarely occurs in its native state; 75 percent of the metal is recovered from gold, lead, and copper ore processing.*

▼ *Platinum smelting has become vital in many industrial applications. The photo shows platinum vaporization.*

◀ *Discovered by the Spanish in Colombia, platinum is the rarest of the precious metals. The meter used as the standard unit of length and its copies are made of this metal.*

▲ *Proustite. An important silver-bearing ore, made up of up to 65 percent of precious metal. Proustite, along with pyrargyrite, belongs to the "red" silvers.*

◀ *Native silver. Each year 9,950 tons of silver are mined from underground. The major producer is Mexico.*

▲ *After a preparatory stage, gold is placed in a crucible and put in an oven to be melted.*

▶ *At Annecy, France, the last gold beaters in Europe still make gold leaf in the traditional way. Here we see the preparatory stage.*

Five Thousand Years of Jewelry Making

▲ *In the oven, gold begins to melt at 1,063°C (1,945°F).*

▼ *A foundry worker pours liquid gold into a mold.*

Because of its sunny sparkle, gold has been an object of admiration from the earliest prehistoric times. Later, the Egyptians created a cult of it, through the famous golden calf, the sacred representation of Ra, the sun god. The earliest humans collected it from the soil or from river sands, and flattened the pebbles to make adornments. They had discovered one of the great properties of the yellow metal: its exceptional malleability. In fact, it is the most malleable of all metals, along with silver, aluminum, and copper. It can be reduced to sheets one thousandth of a millimeter (0.00004 in.) thick by simple hammering. Gold leaf is used in all types of art; it is used to gild nonprecious metals such as bronze to protect them from oxidation, because gold is perfectly unalterable in water and air. Gold also is highly ductile; a single gram (0.035 oz.) of the precious metal can be made into a wire 3,500 m (11,480 ft.) long, without breaking. Gold wire obtained in this way is traditionally used in soft furnishings, such as curtains. Hammering led the way to the fabrication of the first gold vessels around 2500 B.C. in Anatolia; this was the beginning of gold tableware. Metallurgy, also begun in Anatolia, includes the technique of molding. Gold has a low fusion point, 1,063°C (1,945°F), even lower than that of copper. It is the first metal that man was able to melt and pour.

▲ *A gold beater pounds the precious metal to reduce it to a sheet.*

▲ *Gold leaf obtained by pounding. Gold, the most malleable of metals, had been worked from pebbles by prehistoric people. Because of its malleability, it can be reduced to a sheet less than a thousandth of a millimeter (0.00004 in.) thick.*

▶ *Edge gilding. Gold is traditionally used in various art endeavors, such as in gilding the edges or plates of books, illumination, jewelry, of course, metalworking, and even textiles.*

▼ *Gold laminated by machine. One of the qualities of gold is that it is the most malleable of metals. In fact, 1 g (0.035 oz.) can be stretched to 3.5 km (2.17 mi.) without breaking.*

◀ *Pre-Columbian gold statuette. All civilizations have revered gold. In South America, it was compared to the sun god because of its brilliance.*

▼ *Gold leaf for gold gilding and wood gilding is carefully placed between sheets of paper prior to being sold.*

▲ *These gold-plated disks are indispensable for using an electronic microscope, where they will be a critical lens element.*

▼ *Gold has important uses in industrial, scientific, and medical fields. Here, gold is vaporized for the electron microscope.*

29

Minerals, Makeup, and Pigments

▲ *The Arabs still use stibnite reduced to powder to color their eyelids. This is the famous kohl, whose name in Arabic means antimony.*

▶ *Stibnite on quartz. The black of the stibnite is due to the antimony it contains. Egyptian women used it as eye makeup in ancient times.*

▲ *Cerussite crystals with barite. The Romans extracted white from ceruse, a lead mineral they thought to be cerussite.*

▼ *The lead white obtained from cerussite was outlawed in 1905 because it was very toxic. It has been replaced in paint by the white from zinc.*

The first paintings done on the walls of caves (Lascaux in France, Altamira in Spain) are about 15,000 years old. Scenes of bison hunting, among others, show pictures full of color. To obtain this color, Cro-Magnon man used pigments, minerals reduced to powder, or organic substances for painting, for dyeing cloth, and for face paint. Ocher, a friable clay, yellow, brown, or red according to the type of oxides it contains, provided the primary colors. Pigments are also used for body paint, as seen later among the American Indians. In ancient times, new pigments enriched the palette, such as the colors used in the frescoes of Pompeii. The reds come from cinnabar and realgar, the blues from azurite, the greens from chromite, the whites from ceruse, the yellow from orpiment (its Latin name, *auri pigmen-*

tum means "golden color"). Black was derived from stibnite, an antimony mineral. The Romans used it as eyeshadow, using green powder from malachite to contour the eyes, and hematite or cinnabar for lip color.

During the Middle Ages, lapis lazuli appeared. It was brought from the Orient during the fifth century and produced the precious ultramarine blue. Later, minium, a red pigment from lead oxide, was used as a rust inhibitor. Even the silver gray that the masters of the Renaissance prized so highly comes from argentite. The appearance during the nineteenth century of synthetic pigments based on hydrocarbons expanded the palette, but even today we still use minerals to give color: celestine, traditionally mined for its white pigment, is used today as a welcome escape from synthetics in reds and yellows.

▲ *Hematite (or oligist). Prehistoric artists used red from hematite; the hematite can be seen on frescoes in the caves at Lascaux, France (13,000 B.C.).*

▲ *The red of hematite is caused by iron oxide. It is still used in painting under the name of Indian red.*

▼ Azurite with malachite. When azurite is reduced to a powder, it gives a blue pigment that has been used in painting and dyeing since ancient times.

▲ A natural pigment, formerly extracted from lapis lazuli, was ultramarine blue. It was replaced in 1826 by a synthetic blue.

▲ Azurite with malachite. Azurite pigment produces shades of blue, from the lightest to the darkest.

◄ Azurite with cuprite. The blue color of the azurite is due to its high copper content. Copper is a metal that is associated more with the color red.

Cinnabar Red

The vermilion red extracted from cinnabar (at the left, with drops of mercury) was the pigment most often used in ancient times, along with red ocher. For the Romans, it was a sacred color. The bodies of conquering generals were symbolically smeared with cinnabar upon their entry into Rome, as a sign of a great blood victory.

▼ Celestite on sulfur. Celestite (sometimes called celestine) produces an extremely dazzling carmine red. It is used for fireworks and also for distress flares.

▼ Here we see barite with fluorite. Barite is now used as a pigment in paint; in particular, it produces barium yellow.

▲ Stibnite. The antimony obtained from stibnite is still used in the cosmetic industry.

◄ Radiating barite. Barium, a silvery white metal contained in barite is the reason for its numerous applications as a pigment.

▶ The red of celestite is due to the metal it contains called strontium. Celestine, however, is naturally white or yellow.

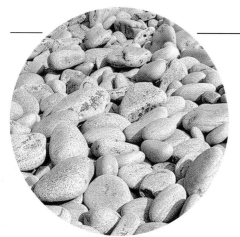

▲ *Polished and made round by the movement of water, pebbles are commonly used in construction. Crushed and incorporated into cement, they produce concrete.*

▼ *Sorting pebbles on the shore of Crotoy, in the Bay of Somme, France. Up until the last century, pebbles and flint were in great demand for use as gunflint.*

▼ *Pebbles collected in Crotoy are roasted in an oven in order to reduce them to powder.*

Minerals and Architecture

For at least 10,000 years, stone has been the best material to use to build houses. It measures up well to cement and to glass facades. It can be obtained by merely cutting it from the inexhaustible amount of rocks that are found on the surface of the earth. Magmatic rocks, created by the crystallization of magma, provide the hardest materials—basalt, rhyolite, and granite. The abbey of Mont-Saint-Michel, in France, is one of the most beautiful examples of granite architecture. Granite is less often used today in building, but it is still indispensable for road maintenance work, although softer rocks are also used.

Slate is a black schist, which, because of its structure, can be split into thin slabs that are ideal for roofs because it is resistant to bad weather. Sedimentary rocks, which are easy to cut, are most often used in building.

Sandstones, made up of sand and feldspars, are in particular demand when they are colored red by iron oxides. Baked to 1,300°C (2,372°F), they can also be used like clay for making tiles. Limestone, a sedimentary rock made up of calcite, provides significant construction materials, from concrete blocks to marble.

The Romans already knew how to burn limestone to make chalk. They mixed it with sand to make mortar, the binding material for their engineering works. Limestone also produces cement; it must be crushed with clay and heated to 1,500°C (2,732°F). Concrete is produced by mixing cement with water, sand, and gravel. Heating gypsum to 150°C (302°F) dehydrates it to produce plaster, a process already known to the Egyptians 5,000 years before our time.

▲ *Crotoy, on the Bay of Somme in France, is home to the last pebble collectors in the world. An activity born with the cut stone industry, it is millions of years old.*

◀▶ *When it comes out of the oven, the pebble powder is white. It is used in road maintenance as a resurfacing agent and also in toothpaste.*

▼ *Limestone rocks located along the coasts (here, we see them in Crete) provide important construction materials, from marble to concrete blocks.*

▲ *Traditional roofing with "lauze," a rock used for centuries in the south of France.*

◄ *Extremely abundant in the south of France, "lauze" is a schist similar to slate. It is cut into plates for covering the roofs of traditional houses because it is resistant to bad weather.*

▶ *Calcite is the primary constituent of limestone. When crushed with clay and heated to 1,500°C (2,732°F), it becomes cement.*

▼ *The burning of calcite produces chalk, which, when mixed with water and sand, produces mortar for construction.*

▲ *Heated to between 150 and 200°C (302 and 392°F), gypsum gives up its water and becomes plaster. Every year, 60 million tons of this mineral are used for building.*

▶ *A shepherd's hut in France, made of limestone material found in the southern part of France.*

▼ *Facade in the Causses, in southern France. "Causse" means a limestone plateau, derived from the Latin calx, like chalk and calcite.*

▲ *Like most of the religious buildings of the Middle Ages, St. Stephen's Cathedral of Vienna (Austria) is constructed of granite.*

◄ *Here is an Aztec pyramid in Tenochtitlan, now Mexico, built during the fourteenth and fifteenth centuries out of limestone blocks.*

Marble and Statuary

▲ Calcite
on fluorite
and sphalerite.
Marble is a metamorphosed
limestone made up of finely crystallized calcite.

▼ White calcite with dioptase. The mirrorlike appearance
of marble after polishing gave it its name, from the Greek
marmaros, "shiny rock."

▲ Calcite with duftite. Calcite that produces marble also
makes up travertine, a calcareous tufa that is used in
construction.

▲ Cliffs of the Bay of Somme (France). Created by sedimentation at the bottom of the sea, limestone provides precious materials for
sculpture, such as marble.

P rehistoric man used flint points to carve limestone, to try to give three-dimensional shape to their artistic and spiritual work.

The Venus of Willendorf and other works of art are evidence of statuettes that are more than 20,000 years old associated with the most ancient fertility cults. Of all limestones, marble rapidly became the preferred material. Its low degree of hardness gave the sculptor unparalleled ease of cutting, along with the ability to polish it, which gave it its Greek name of marmaros ("shiny rock"). The marbles of Paros and Carrara give an impression of white "antique" marble, but it can also be spotted, veined, or jaspered, or variously colored according to the impurities it contains. There is also blue Turquin marble, yellow marble from Sienna, black St. Laurent marble, serpentine green (or ophitic) marble, and pink marble from China. Rocks less easy to work with than marble are also used for sculpture, including granite, basalt, or porphyry, a semiprecious material much admired for its variety of red, and named after porphuritês (Greek for "purple stone").

Metal sculpture, a tradition as old as that of marble, is linked to gold and silver working in classical antiquity. The Egyptians had erected two obelisks made of electrum, a natural alloy of gold and silver, in front of their temple of Thebes. Each obelisk weighed 40 tons. Less likely to attract the greedy, bronze quickly replaced these materials to decorate gardens and public places.

▲ Bas-relief in marble in the Alhambra in Grenada,
Spain.
▶ The Alhambra of Grenada. The thirteenth-century
Moorish masterpiece is made entirely of marble.

◀ *The statues of Easter Island are 10 m (33 ft.) high. Related to totems of other Polynesian islands, they bear witness to ancient megalithic cults.*

▲ *Easter Island, in Polynesia, is famous for its statues carved from basalt, a volcanic rock. The hats are pink granite.*

◀ *Three-quarters of the statues of Easter Island now lie on the ground; however, there is currently an ambitious UNESCO program that seeks to set them upright again.*

▲ *Cromlech in Stonehenge (England), a megalithic monument in sandstone from the Bronze Age, probable evidence of an ancient solar cult.*
▼ *White "antique" marble still inspires statuary.*

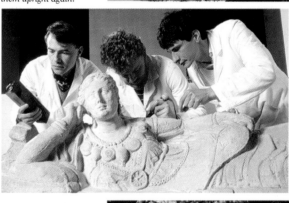

◀◀ *Marble resists the test of time. Collecting samples in the Louvre Museum in Paris for carbon 14 dating of antique statues.*
▼ *Bronze statue of Johann Strauss gilded with gold (Vienna, Austria). Bronze is gilded with gold leaf, with mercury or by electroplating.*

Bronze Working

Bronze is a man-made alloy made up of 90 percent copper and 10 percent tin. It was invented in the Orient 5,000 years ago, by reaction of a tin oxide, cassiterite, with copper ore. Used very often in antique statues, its use expanded throughout most of the decorative arts from the eighteenth century on, especially in the ornamentation of buildings or the manufacture of precious objects. To avoid oxidation, it is gilded or patinated in brown, black, or green called "antique" (to the left, the patinated bronze statue of the poet and dramatist Goethe, in Vienna, Austria).

35

▲ *Rock crystal quartz. Glass was invented in Egypt in about 3500 B.C., but transparency was not achieved until the fifth century B.C.*

▼ *Muscovite mica, fuchsine variety. Muscovite is still used for high temperature ovens because it is much more resistant to heat than glass.*

Glass and Ceramics

The oldest shards of pottery have been found in Jericho, in the Middle East. They make it possible to date the appearance of ceramics at around 8000 B.C. The word comes from the Greek *keramas*, which means clay, a very common soil type produced by the desegregation of sedimentary rocks under water. Mixed with water, sand, and feldspar, it has the property of hardening in an oven at 800°C (1,472°F). The baked earth obtained in this way is the most simple ceramic, that of our familiar flowerpots, and also the most breakable. By exploiting the varieties of clay (calcareous or ferruginous), and subjecting them to higher temperatures, it is also possible to obtain finer, more delicate, more resistant ceramics such as terra-cotta, earthenware, stoneware, or even porcelain. The invention of glass follows directly that of ceramics. It is probably from the Egyptians, around 3500 B.C. and is the first material that man obtained by chemical synthesis. At its base, quartz or a sand rich in silica is heated to fusion between 1,300 and 1,600°C (2,372–2,912°F). Soda and chalk must be added to the formula or the paste produced will turn out to be soluble in water.

Transparent glass was not achieved until the fifth century B.C. by the Persians, while in Rome the technique of blown glass was developed, replacing ceramics and metal for making receptacles. Cooling glass on a flat surface to make glass sheets has been known since ancient times; this technique would continue to improve until the seventeenth century, leading to the development of mirrors and windowpanes. The glass industry today provides very fire-resistant materials whose uses have been expanded to household use, as with fluorosilicates, borosilicates, such as Pyrex, or even ceramic glass found in the portholes of space shuttles.

▲ *Phlogopite mica with albite. Less transparent than muscovite, phlogopite is used as an insulating material in electrical equipment.*

▼ *Rock crystal quartz. Silica in the form of rock crystal or sand makes up 75 percent of the composition of glass.*

▲ *Mica with cleavelandite albite. The transparent varieties of mica were used for a long time as windowpanes, before glass became common.*

▲ The sparkle of crystal, much greater than that of glass, is due to the presence of lead oxide (minium) in the formula. Seen here, the celebrated Baccarat crystal plant, in France.

▲ From the eleventh century, Venetian masters have excelled in the production of opaque glass that looks like porcelain, chalcedony, and agate.

Porcelain Earth

Kaolinite is the principal constituent of kaolin, a white clay that produces porcelain when baked at 1,400°C (2,552°F), hence its name "porcelain earth." Porcelain is a Chinese invention taken to Europe by Marco Polo. Porcelain was then as valuable as gold, because the Chinese jealously guarded the secret of its manufacture, which was not revealed until the eighteenth century when kaolin deposits were discovered in Europe. This was the beginning of the Saxe and Limoges porcelain industries.

▼ Founded in 1764, the Baccarat crystal factory is known worldwide for the artistic quality of its creations. Seen here, gilding on crystal.

▼ Lead crystal is a seventeenth-century English invention. It quickly replaced white glass, also known as Bohemia crystal.

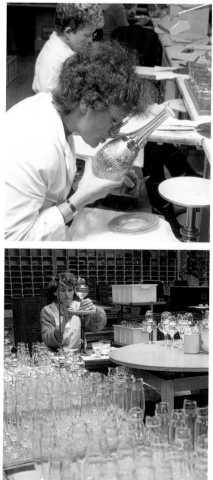

▼ Ceramic glass is a very resistant glass that is used in space shuttles. Here, the fabrication of a lens for a particle accelerator.

▲ Working in glass makes it possible to create minute reconstructions of marine animals (nautiloids) from fossils.

◀ Crystal art makes use of materials as diverse as precious opals, alabaster, sulfides, and millefiori, not to mention white glass.

Industrial Minerals

▲ *A piece of flint. Flint has the property of breaking into blades with sharp edges. These were formidable weapons for men in prehistoric times.*

▶ *Paleolithic and neolithic tools. The neolithic, the last period of the Stone Age, began around 8000 B.C. with polished stone and terra-cotta.*

▲ *Around 2.5 million years ago, Homo habilis began to break pebbles to make tools; this is the beginning of the Paleolithic, or second period of the Stone Age.*

▶ *Neolithic arrowhead. The neolithic was marked by the thinning of flint into almond-shaped points. Arrows, knives, and hatchets appeared.*

◀ *Scrapers, bevels, primitive hand axes— Paleolithic man made tools out of stone that were quite superior to previous ones made of bone or wood.*

▶ *The discovery of Homo habilis at the site of Olduvai (Tanzania) in 1953 revealed a stone industry with tools that had already been well developed, from which came the name "skillful man."*

Minerals and Civilization

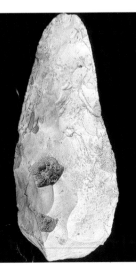

Everything started 2.5 million years ago when *Homo habilis*, a man with a receding forehead, began to break flint nodules that he collected in rivers. He discovered their ability to be made into long, sharp blades, unfortunately for the 4 m-long (12 ft.) glyptodon that encountered the 10 cm (4 in.) of deadly flint. The Stone Age would last more than two million years and man would assure his control of the planet during this time with the help of his most solid ally: stone. Stone was not only cut but also polished or fired to make pottery, from 8000 B.C. (neothithic).

A new level of civilization was reached in the Orient around 4500 B.C. with the invention of metallurgy. Copper metallurgy came first, and men learned to extract copper from malachite by reduction over charcoal. Melting at 1,083°C (1,900°F), it was used to make very effective weapons. The technique was completed around 3400 B.C. by the manufacture of bronze, copper reinforced with tin, the first metallic alloy made by man. Iron metallurgy began around 2600 B.C. Iron had been known for a long time for its hardness and its lightness, but it was not used on a large scale because it could rarely be found in a pure state. Reduction of limonite by fire soon provided access to inexhaustible reserves of iron ore.

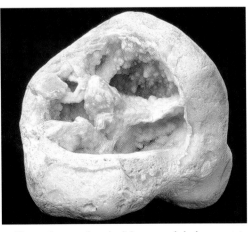

▲ *Flint, a siliceous rock made of almost pure chalcedony occurs in nodules among river pebbles.*

From Pyrite to Fire

By pounding flint on pyrite (left), Homo erectus domesticated fire 730,000 years ago. When pounded, pyrite gives off sparks that can set twigs on fire, an enormous leap in progress that would lead to ceramics, then metallurgy. In their day, the Romans lit their fires by scraping a nail on pyrite.

▼ Fluorite. Necklaces of fluorite beads more than two million years old have been found in Belgium. These are some of the first jewels.

▼ Gold nugget. Attracted to its sparkle, prehistoric man collected gold from the ground and beat it with pebbles to make it into adornments.

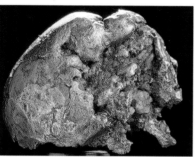

◀ Very abundant in nature, colored quartz was used as adornments by prehistoric man.

▶ Venus of Willendorf. This statuette (11 cm–4.29 in.), discovered in Austria, was carved from limestone. It shows the advanced art in the late Paleolithic period.

◀ Native copper. The Copper Age appeared in the Orient around 4500 B.C., when man learned to melt copper (1,083°C–1,900°F) and pour it into molds.

▲ Venus of Laussel, also called "Venus of Berlin." Neolithic stone Venuses were probably fertility goddesses.

◀ Bronze mask. Around 3400 B.C. man invented bronze, a very resistant alloy of copper and tin that did not exist in nature.

▼ Limonite (with adamite). Not found in its native state, iron was first obtained by reducing natural oxides, such as limonite, by fire.

▲ Iron ore (siderite). The metallurgy of iron started in Anatolia around 2600 B.C., making it possible to produce higher performance weapons than those made of copper.

◀ Malachite. Metallurgists learned to extract copper from malachite by reduction with charcoal. They made weapons and adornments from it.

Native copper. Its name comes from the Latin cuprium, *which referred to the island of Cyprus, one of the important ancient production areas, along with Andalusia.*

Siderite and dolomite, with pyrrhotite. Extracted from ore, iron is the most common industrial metal; 700 million tons of it are produced each year, especially for steel.

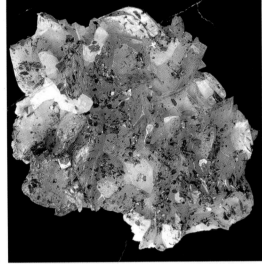

Metallic Ores

In spite of the recent revolution in plastic, metals are the most commonly used industrial materials. These are simple substances—not alloys—characterized by high density and malleability that permit them to be shaped by simple hammering. Minerals that don't contain metals are rare. Those that abound in them are called ores when they can be used profitably. Gold, silver, copper, tin, iron, lead, mercury, and zinc are the oldest metals known; they have been known since ancient times. The oldest industrial metal is copper, which has been recovered from ores for 6,500 years. An excellent conductor, it is used today for the manufacture of electrical cables, with an annual production of 10 million tons.

Lead was used in the pipes of Roman sewers, a role it still plays because of its resistance to corrosion. Zinc was known in ancient times only as brass, a copper alloy. Its use as a roof covering goes back only about a century.

Pillar of the Industrial Revolution in the nineteenth century, iron is definitely the metal most produced (700 million tons per year) in the world. An average consumer uses 500 kg (1,100 lb.) per year, from car to canned food.

Hematite (or oligist). Burned in an oven, the ferrous ore is first converted into cast iron, then refined to produce iron or steel; this is called iron and steel metallurgy.

Galena with sphalerite. Galena is the ore that is most exploited for lead today. It is also a significant silver ore.

Extracted from hemimorphite since ancient times, zinc was known in the form of brass, then as a metal in the seventeenth century.

Galena with barite and fluorite on sphalerite. Very rare in its native state, lead has long been extracted from galena.

▶ *Cerussite. This ore was mined by the Romans, who made pipes out of lead for their sewers.*

▼ *Pyromorphite. Malleable when cold, iron was recovered from ores very early in the history of man. In fact, lead statuettes dating back 3,800 years have been found in Egypt.*

▼ *Industrial use of zinc began only in the last century. Extracted from smithsonite, among other ores, it is used for roof covering.*

▼ *Anglesite and galena. Made up of three-fourths lead, anglesite was discovered in Wales (Galles, in French), hence the name.*

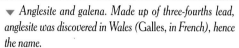

▼ *Tennantite (gray copper). Having excellent thermal conductivity, copper extracted from ore is used for the manufacture of electrical cables.*

▲ *Tetrahedrite (gray copper). This copper ore, more abundant than tennantite, also contains antimony, mercury, and sometimes even silver.*

▲ *Cuprite. An important copper-bearing ore, providing a good part of the 10 million tons of copper that are produced every year.*

▼ *Azurite with cuprite. Copper, extracted from azurite and from cuprite, occurs in many alloys, such as bronze with tin, or brass with zinc.*

▲ *Polymetallic nodules collected from the ocean bottom are the ores of tomorrow. They can satisfy our need for nickel for the next 150,000 years.*

◀ *Cutting a polymetallic nodule. The copper source contained in the polymetallic nodules will be worked for 6,000 years.*

Minerals of the Alchemists

Gold nuggets. The lack of yellow metal that Europe had experienced until the discovery of the New World nourished the alchemist's myth of transmutation into gold. The transmutation of base metals into gold became a quest of the alchemists, a science from ancient Greece and its center, Alexandria (Egypt).

▲ *In search of "quintessence;" alchemists invented the double boiler and the distillation apparatus for the distillation of minerals (shown here, marcasite).*

The alchemists of the Middle Ages were convinced that they would be able to change base metals into gold once they possessed the philosopher's stone; all they had to do was find it. They assumed it was made up of four basic or main elements of all matter: sulfur, mercury, earth, and fire, to which must be added a fifth ingredient of an indeterminate type. Paracelsus, in the sixteenth century, leaned toward arsenic, isolated by alchemists three centuries earlier. Others went in search of magnetite, because of its magnetic properties. A German alchemist thought it might be found in his urine, and in analyzing it, he isolated phosphorus in 1669.

By putting minerals into fire, alchemists hoped to get to the elemental substance, the key to all chemistry. They experimented by melting, causing the solid state to change to the liquid state, and by distillation, which changes the liquid to a vapor state, thereby inventing the distillation apparatus.

In spite of not having laid their hands on the philosopher's stone, alchemists did produce concrete results. In the eighteenth century, sulfuric acid, called oil of vitriol, and nitric acid, called "strong water," were discovered, soon followed by hydrochloric acid ("salt spirit").

▲ *Upon alteration, realgar produces arsenic, an element that was isolated by alchemists during the thirteenth century.*

◀ *Antimony extracted from stibnite was a panacea for the alchemist doctors. They made "eternity pills," purges, and diuretics. This was a dangerous medication, because antimony has properties similar to those of arsenic.*

▶ *Pyrite is similar to gold in appearance and therefore fools many an inexperienced eye, thus its name, "fool's gold."*

◀ *The distillation of sulfur would lead the alchemists to discover sulfuric acid in the thirteenth century, then nitric and hydrochloric acid.*

▶ *Chalcedony, chrysoprase variety. Green stones were considered good for soil fertility, because it was believed they caused rain to fall.*

▲ *Heirs to the Greek esotericism, alchemists venerated rock crystal (quartz), whose transparency was thought to allow them to read the future. This is the origin of crystal balls.*

▲ *Because of its color, powdered red jasper was prescribed by alchemists at one time to stop hemorrhages from wounds.*

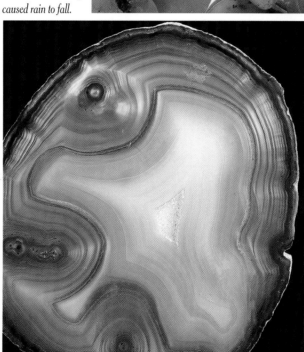

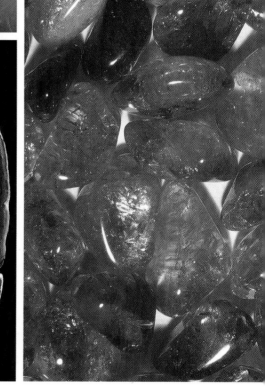

▲ *Paracelsus believed the shape or color of a mineral was an indication of a curative property. Cloudy agate was prescribed for fumigation.*

▲ *Citrines. The yellow stones were thought to cure jaundice and liver ailments.*

▲ *Blue stones (here, chalcedony) related to the clearness of the sky, were supposed to cure eye problems.*

Three Pieces of Lead

From pyromorphite, alchemists extracted lead, which was an important metal that they believed could be turned into gold. As a means of protection, the alchemists would attach three pieces of lead to their clothes: on the heart, the stomach, and the lower abdomen.

▶ *Cobalt-bearing dolomite and duftite. Extracted from cobaltite, cobalt is a very resistant mineral used for the fabrication of special alloys, such as ferrocobalt, among others.*
▼ *Scheelite provides tungsten, which is used for the manufacture of light bulb filaments, among other things. Its amber-colored crystals are often cut as gems.*

Modern Metals

T wo centuries ago, all industry was based on the exploitation of about 20 mineral substances. Today, the number has risen to 80 and three-quarters of them are metals because scientific tools have been refined since the seventeenth century—the microscope appeared, among others—with the result that the list of new materials continues to increase: cobalt (1735), nickel (1751), manganese (1774), chromium (1780), tungsten (1783), uranium (1789), titanium (1791), aluminum (1825). They are not very abundant in nature; their production hardly exceeds several tens of thousands of tons per year, with the exception of aluminum (18.3 million tons), manganese (5 million tons), and titanium (3.5 million tons), which make up the five most used metals, with iron and copper. The least used is radium (100 g–3.5 oz. per year) because of its radioactivity. All these materials have found their place in areas as diverse as petrochemistry, electronics, or aerospace.

Because of its lightness, titanium is used in the fuselages of supersonic aircraft, along with tungsten carbide. In metallurgy, metals are alloyed with steel—ferrochrome, ferrocobalt, ferromolybdenum—to create "special" steel with very high resistance.

▲ *Garnierite is an important ore of nickel, a nonferrous metal discovered in the eighteenth century. The name nickel comes from the German Kupfernickel, "devil's copper."*

Superstition

Ancient people from the North believed there were demons in the mines. The most fearful of these demons were thought to cause explosions and acidic vapors. Others that were less frightening, the Kobolds, borrowed the features of the miners to create disturbances in the mine shafts. From this comes the name of cobaltite, a mineral very abundant in Sweden, where cobalt was discovered in 1735.

▲ *Pyrite octahedron. Pyrite, a very common mineral that is rich in iron, can also contain cobalt.*

▲ *Barite with fluorite. Barium, a metal isolated in 1808, is extracted from barite. It is used to make protective concrete for nuclear power plants.*

◀ *Vanadinite provides vanadium, a nonferrous metal isolated in 1801. Vanadium is very shock-resistant, and is used in valves and springs.*
▼ *Vanadinite. This vanadium ore also provides rhenium, a rare metal isolated in 1925, whose production does not exceed 7 tons per year.*

▲ *Sphalerite. This zinc ore also provides rare metals that were discovered recently, such as thallium (1861), gallium (1875), and germanium (1886).*

◀ *Endlichite is a variety of vanadinite that is rich in arsenic. Arsenic and vanadium are considered very toxic elements.*
▼ *Titanium, a very light and resistant metal, is extracted from rutile. It is used in alloys in the fuselages of supersonic aircraft.*

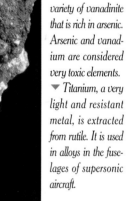

▲ *Extracted from wolframite, tungsten (or wolfram) was isolated in 1783. It is a high-density metal, whose name, of Swedish origin, means "heavy stone."*

◀ *Common beryl is used to make beryllium, a metal used in the aerospace industry.*

▼ *Bauxite. Aluminum is made from this sedimentary rock. It is used in industry (18.3 million tons per year).*

▼ *Tantalite. This is the main ore of tantalum, a light corrosion-resistant metal, that is used to make surgical instruments.*

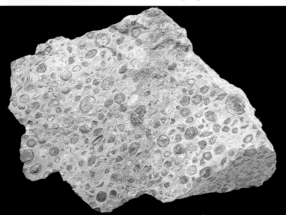

◀ *Molybdenite in quartz. This is the main ore of molybdenum, a white metal similar to chromium. Very resistant, it is used for the manufacture of special steels.*

▲ Extracted from enargite and other ores, arsenic is a metal used in industry to harden lead and to make various alloys. Its production is 47,000 tons per year.

▶ Arsenopyrite with wolframite and quartz. Arsenic is found in the native state, but it is also extracted from arsenopyrite by open-air roasting.

▲ Berthierite is a source of antimony, a semimetallic element. Neither ductile nor malleable, it is not considered a metal, but a metalloid.

Nonmetallic Ores

Three-quarters of the 109 elements inventoried in nature are metals; all the others are nonmalleable solids or gases, therefore, they cannot be used for similar purposes. The importance of these nonmetallic ores is considerable, however; entire areas of economic activity are based on them, for example, building. The manufacture of plaster requires 60 million tons of gypsum per year, and 4 million tons of asbestos are used.

Asbestos is a group of fibrous minerals that are very resistant to fire; to be an ore of asbestos, a rock must contain at least 3 percent asbestos. Quartz from sand, and mica, talc, kaolin, and some quantities of feldspars are necessary ingredients for the production of glass and ceramics.

Mineral acids such as sulfuric, hydrochloric, nitric, or phosphoric acids have opened up a broad field of industrial applications, not much older than a century, such as the manufacture of plastic materials. Sulfuric acid is made from sulfur, which is produced in the amount of 60 million tons per year. About 170 million tons of rock salt are mined for hydrochloric acid and sodium hydroxide, the basis of soaps and detergents. Phosphoric acid is made from phosphates, which come from apatite or guano (bird excrement). Phosphates also provide the majority of the synthetic fertilizers. Natural nitrates provide nitric acid. Like phosphates, they are significant fertilizers; their principal ore is a saline rock from Chile called caliche.

Potassium nitrate is formed on the humid walls of cowsheds; this is saltpeter, "salt from rock," which is the source of gunpowder. Today, it is still mined but for more sophisticated explosives, of the nitroglycerine type.

▶ Abundant when it is in its native state, sulfur is also extracted from ores (seen here, galena). It is used to make the sulfuric acid found in detergents.

◀ Seen here, stibnite. Antimony has properties similar to those found in arsenic. It is used in the manufacture of batteries for automobiles.

Asbestos

Taken from its Latin name asbestos, which means "incombustible," asbestos includes several fibrous minerals known since ancient times for their resistance to fire. Egyptians wove it into shrouds for the pharoahs. These minerals are still used under the industrial name, asbestos. Crocidolite (shown at the right) provides asbestos with long fibers that are used to make firefighting suits.

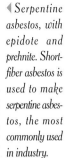

◀ Serpentine asbestos, with epidote and prehnite. Short-fiber asbestos is used to make serpentine asbestos, the most commonly used in industry.

▶ Violet fluorite with grains of quartz. Fluoride, which is used in toothpaste, is best known for its ability to prevent cavities.

▼ Violet fluorite. Freon, a derivative of fluoride, has refrigerant properties that are used in freezers and air-conditioning systems.

▼ Violet fluorite. Fluorite, which is best known in industry by the name of "fluorspar," is the source of fluorine, a gas that was not isolated until 1886.

▲ Black fluorite. Fluorine derivatives make up propellant gases in aerosols that contribute to the destruction of the ozone layer.

▼ Phosphorus, a nonmetallic solid, is extracted from apatite. It gives off light in contact with air and was used in the invention of matches in 1830.

▲ Native sulfur is a product of volcanic activity. It was used long ago, mixed with saltpeter, to make black powder, the oldest explosive used by mankind.

▶ *Zircon, seen here, is the source of two rare metals: zirconium and hafnium. They are both used in nuclear reactions.*

▼ *Autunite is an important ore of uranium, the metal in which radioactivity was discovered in 1896 by the French physicist Henri Becquerel.*

Minerals of the Atomic Age

Industrial civilization was first based on the exploitation of energy sources found underground: coal, petroleum, natural gas. These are actually fossil fuels, produced by the decomposition of ancient organisms; however, looking into the very heart of matter, a new energy source called radioactivity was discovered in 1896. Radioactivity exists naturally in almost 240 minerals, such as pitchblende, torbernite, monazite, or autunite, which are strongly discouraged for mineral collections. All are made up of heavy metals, of the uranium, thorium, radium, or actinium type. Very unstable, these elements disintegrate spontaneously into new species, both lighter and more stable. In the course of this process, which takes place over millions of years, they release considerable energy as radiation. The possibility of artificially reproducing this phenomenon can produce nuclear—etymologically, that which is released from the nucleus of an atom—energy on a large scale.

Today, hundreds of radioactive elements are produced in nuclear cells, the most common being natural uranium. The energy that is thus obtained is converted into electricity in power plants; it is also used to propel submarines or to make satellites work. All this is not without effects on man and his environment. Radioactivity acts by radiation—the effect of radiation on organisms—which can cause serious lesions, even genetic abnormalities. It also creates contamination, as in radon, a very toxic radioactive gas that is produced by the disintegration of radium, which is deposited in the lungs. People in some cities are beginning to find radon in the air in alarming amounts.

On the other hand, the destructive effects of radiation are used beneficially in the medical world; for example, radiotherapy is used for the treatment of cancer, using cobalt isotope 60, which is a cobalt therapy unit.

▲ *Uranium present in autunite (seen here, green by fluorescence) spontaneously disintegrates, creating an energy source: radioactivity.*

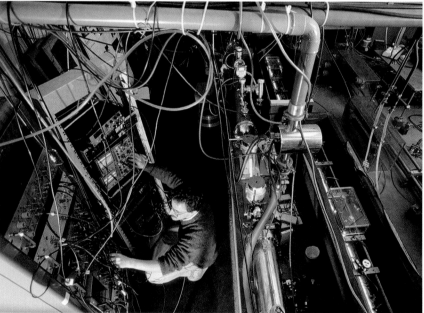

▲ *The vibrations of the cesium (a metal) atom are used for atomic clocks. Atomic clocks have regulated international time since 1971.*
◀ *Because of the high density of barite (4.5), it is used in protective concrete to neutralize radiation around nuclear power plants.*
▶ *Around the world, 200 atomic clocks keep time with a precision greater than a billionth of a second. Here, the clock in the Paris observatory.*

▼ A natural radioactive source causes the color of smoky quartz. About 240 minerals are radioactive, to a more or less dangerous degree.

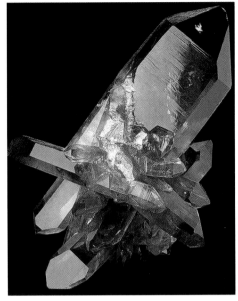

▼ Out of the 39,000 tons of lithium produced from lepidolite every year, a large part is used in electronics to make television screens.

▲ Tungsten (or wolfram), a metal used for fuel in spacecraft, is extracted from wolframite.

▶ Rare metals that are not abundant in nature, such as yttrium, lanthanum, and scandium, are necessary for lasers to function.

▲ Lepidolite, a mica, is a source of lithium. It is the least dense metal (0.55), and is used to make nuclear bombs.

◀ Among other peacetime applications, nuclear power plants today also provide a significant amount of electricity.

▶ Here we see sphalerite with dolomite. Gallium, which is a rare metal that is extracted from sphalerite, is used in lasers as a semiconductor.

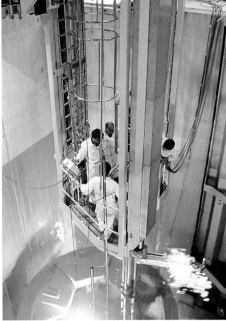

▲ At this research center in France, the worst catastrophic scenarios are anticipated.

◀ The terrible risk of nuclear accidents makes it essential to train special rescue teams in power plants. At this research center in France, where a nuclear power plant school is located, these simulations take place in an environment that is nonradioactive.

▲ *Fluorine. Fluoride intoxication, or fluorosis, causes asthenia and weight loss. In its acute form, it causes respiratory problems and death.*

▼ *Fluorine. Its gas, used as a propellant in aerosols, is a major polluter that is responsible for the destruction of the ozone layer.*

Careful, Poison!

Some minerals are both therapeutically beneficial and extremely toxic—it all depends on the dose. Mercury salts were used in the Middle Ages and later to cure nervous disorders and syphilis; however, their ingestion can cause serious neurological problems, fetal deformity, or death. Therefore, their use was discontinued in 1941 in favor of penicillin, which had been discovered several years earlier.

Arsenic is another case. We have about 18 milligrams (0.00063 oz.) in our bodies, as a trace element that acts as a stimulant on the organism, but a dose of 50 milligrams is deadly. Arsenic acid, produced from arsenic, is used as an insecticide, and until recently, as an antiseptic in medicine. Used by poisoners and other criminals, crime by arsenic does not pay, as the element adheres to the fingernails, skin, or hair of the victim. The coroner's first examination always aims to detect the presence of arsenic.

Industrial activity based on mineral exploitation is itself beset by a whole series of adverse effects. Miners who extract the ore are the first affected, developing many professional diseases, such as silicosis, which is caused by the repeated inhalation of silica, from their contact with ore. Mineral fertilizers of the nitrate or phosphate type have proven to be powerful poisons of flora and fauna when their wastes have been dumped into the ocean; not to mention radioactive minerals with unknown amounts of fallout that could continue for generations to come. Asbestos used in buildings is the same type of industrial material whose usefulness is equal to its danger. Inhalation of its dust causes pulmonary diseases and thousands of deaths each year. Mined since 1847, today it is prohibited in almost all countries.

▲ *Barite. Baritosis is a disease that affects miners. It is caused by the repeated inhalation of barite dust, which attacks the lungs.*

▼ *Recommended for the use in fumigation since ancient times, burned sulfur is a disinfectant but also pollutes the atmosphere; it is the source of acid rain.*

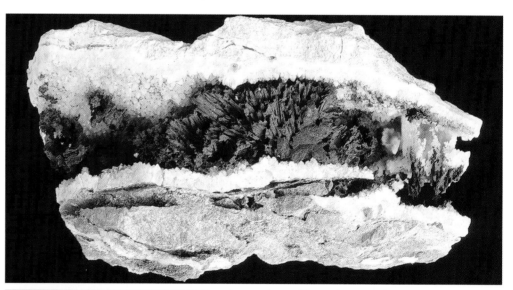

▲ *Arsenopyrite (arsenic ore). Arsenic is naturally present in the human body as a trace element (18 mg–0.00063 oz. on average).*

▲ *Arsenic with rammelsbergite. Arsenic in itself is not dangerous. But its oxide, arsenic oxide, is lethal to the body at a dose of 50 mg (0.00175 oz.).*

▼ *Orpiment (arsenic ore). Arsenic has the property of becoming concentrated in fingernails or hair, which allows criminologists to easily detect it.*

▶*Actinolite asbestos (asbestos). Pro-hibited in many countries throughout the world, asbestos has been replaced by substitutes such as fiberglass.*

◀*Serpentine asbestos (asbestos). Repeated inhalation of asbestos fibers has been proven to cause a deadly pulmonary disease, asbestosis, which is called amiantosis in Canada.*

▲ *Calcination of chlorides (shown here, atacamite) produces hydrochloric acid, the salt spirit used by the ancient alchemists; it should be handled carefully with tweezers.*

Antimony

Legend has it that an alchemist monk once gave antimony to his pigs (above, stibnite, antimony ore). Because the pigs seemed to gain strength from it, he decided to repeat the experiment with his fellow monks. They all died because antimony is often combined with arsenic. This is the doubtful origin of the word antimony, or antimoine in French (moine means "monk" in French).

▲ *Actinolite asbestos (asbestos). In the United States, asbestos dust is responsible for thousands of deaths each year from lung cancer.*

◀*Roasting molybdenite produces sulfur, which can then be converted into sulfuric acid, or vitriol.*

▼ *Autunite is a radioactive mineral that emits a very toxic gas called radon, which concentrates in the lungs. It occurs in alarming concentrations in the air of large cities.*

▲ *Vanadinite is a mineral containing yellowish, brownish, or red crystals that provide vanadium, a metal used in industry to make valves. It must be handled with care because it is highly toxic.*

Minerals
for Life

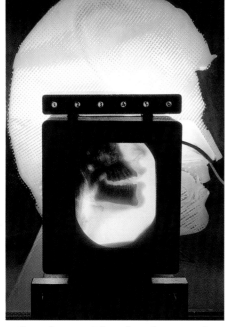

▲ *Our teeth are essentially made up of apatite, a calcium phosphate that is abundant in rocks.*

▼ *Apatite is rich in phosphorus, which is an element present in our bodies in the amount of 500 g (1.1 lb.) on average.*

▼ *Dolomite on sphalerite. Dolomite contains magnesium, the most abundant metal present in the form of an element in the human body (30 g–1.05 oz. on average).*

Minerals in the Body

The human body contains an average of 13 kg (28.6 lb.) of carbon. Carbon is the most abundant mineral in the body. Through photosynthesis, carbon plays a role that is comparable to silicon in rocks; this is why organic chemistry can also be called carbon chemistry. Calcium is almost the only constituent of our bones and our bodies contain at least 1 kg (2.2 lb.) of it. It is also present in oyster and snail shells.

Looking more closely, our teeth are just phosphorus combined with calcium, a finely crystallized phosphate, that is very similar to the mineral apatite that is found in rocks. Many other metals and metalloids are revealed by analysis, but in quantities so small that they are called "trace elements." Although 1 g (0.035 oz.) of iron, zinc, silicon, and copper are present in the body, when we talk about manganese, nickel, cobalt, iodine, selenium, chromium, molybdenum, tin, vanadium, aluminum, arsenic, even silver and gold, we are talking about only a thousandth of a gram (0.000035 oz.).

The weight of all these trace elements together is not more than 7 g (0.245 oz.), but their action is of the utmost importance to our metabolism. Iron is the principal constituent of hemoglobin; by itself, it ensures the transport of oxygen into our tissues by the blood. Copper, zinc, and selenium regulate enzyme action, iodine regulates hormones, and cobalt produces vitamin B_{12}. A lack of these elements in the body results in serious functional difficulties, such as loss of vitality, loss of immune defenses, even death. Their contribution through nutrition, when carefully balanced, promotes good physical and psychological health.

Recent discoveries have established that selenium is effective against aging by protecting the cell membrane from oxidation, which would also make it an active agent against cancer. The new science of the biochemistry of minerals still has a great deal to teach us.

◀ *Dolomite with calcite, quartz, and sphalerite. Dolomite and calcite contain calcium, an element indispensable for human neuro-muscular activity.*

◀ *Dolomite. The metallic element magnesium contained in our bodies is a powerful regulator of cardiac rhythm. It also acts on our nervous system.*

▶ *The human skeleton is a mineral structure that is composed of 99 percent calcium.*

◀ *Calcium, shown here, is naturally present in gypsum. It is also present in our bodies and plays a prominent role in the coagulation of blood.*

▼ *Siderite on calcite. Iron, which is present in siderite, is an essential component of hemoglobin. It ensures the oxygenation of tissues.*

▲ *The calcareous exterior of shells is made up primarily of calcite.*

▼ *Trace elements act on metabolism, ensuring our physical and psychological equilibrium. The majority are metals; their total weight in the body does not exceed 7 g (0.245 oz).*

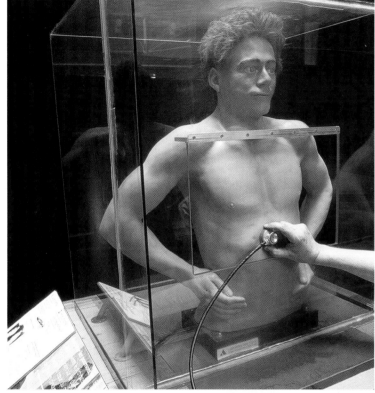

▼ *Chalcopyrite with malachite. Sulfur, which is present in chalcopyrite, is a trace element that occurs in certain amino acids, which are the essential building blocks of protein.*

▼ *Galena and calcite. Lead extracted from galena is also present in our bodies in minute amounts (less than a thousandth of a gram–0.000035 oz.).*

◀ *Manganese, extracted from rhodochrosite, is a very common metal used in industry, along with iron, aluminum, and copper. It is also a trace element.*

▲ *Galena on sphalerite. Zinc from sphalerite is present in the body in an amount almost equal to iron (3.2 g– 0.112 oz.).*

▶ *Violet fluorite with a galena crystal. Fluorine is a trace element that has poorly understood properties.*

▶ *Mountain of salt at Salins-de-Giraud, in southern France.*
▼ *The world production of salt is 170 million tons per year. The primary producing countries are the United States and China.*

▲ *Salt is an important and basic industrial raw material; two-thirds of salt production go into the production of chloride.*

▲ *Ice crystals on a window. Is water a mineral? It all depends on the temperature. At 0°C (32°F), water, which is an oxide, attains a solid state.*

The Salt of Life

Our familiar table salt is a mineral that current nomenclature calls rock salt, or halite. Its beautiful transparent crystals contain 60 percent chlorine and 40 percent sodium, in the form of sodium chloride. Everyone has had the experience of its principal property by sprinkling it on soup, for instance; it dissolves instantly and releases a tangy flavor that is so pleasant to the palate that man has developed the habit of using it to enhance bland foods. Salt is naturally present in the oceans at a concentration of 35 g per L of water (3.5 percent by wt.). It is extracted from shallow basins called salt marshes. It is also found as a solid underground, where it was created by the evaporation of ancient seas, sometimes in beds 200 m (656 ft.) thick.

Prehistoric man used salt to preserve meat or cauterize wounds, because chlorine has a strong bacteria-killing ability. Numerous civilizations have even used it as currency. In fact, Romans paid their armies with salt rations called *salarium;* this is the origin of the word "salary." Salt money was used among the people of the Sahara up until recently. More precious than gold in the desert, salt, when added to food, prevents dehydration.

The decomposition of salt from an electric current (electrolysis) produces chlorine, which is used in industrial markets, especially for the production of detergents. Out of the 170 million tons of salt produced every year, two-thirds of it go to industry, the rest to our tables.

▼ *One-third of world salt production is obtained by the evaporation of seawater in salt marshes, as seen here.*

◀ *Chloride is a gas that is extracted from rock salt. Its derivatives are used in detergents as whitening agents and disinfectants.*

▶ *Aerial view of salt marshes at Aigues-Mortes, in Le Gard, France, where salt is produced.*

▼ *The color red, characteristic of these salt marshes in Le Gard, France, is due to the growth of microorganisms from the sea.*

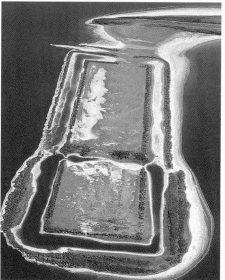

▲ *Salt is necessary for life in the desert, because it acts as protection against dehydration. For this reason, for a long time, it was exchanged as money in the Sahara.*

▲ *Roman legionnaires received a ration of salt called a salarium as payment, which gave rise to the term "salary." Later, they were paid in coins.*

Salt Sculpture

Wieliczka, Poland, possesses the most extraordinary salt mines in the world (right, a block of rock salt). In the mine galleries, which are several meters (1 meter = 3 ft.) deep, miners have carved a whole series of statues and bas-reliefs into the layers of salt. These treasures will never see daylight, because the humidity of the air would immediately destroy them.

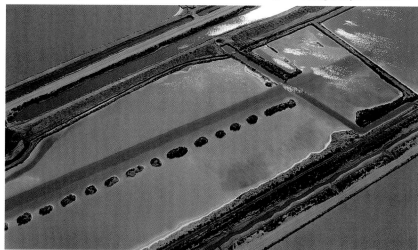

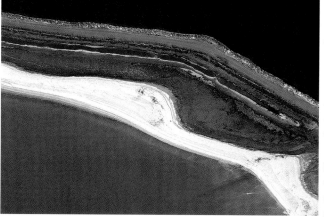

▲ *Javel water, a powerful French disinfectant, was invented in 1795, from chloride. Its name comes from the village, today a Paris neighborhood, where the first factory was opened.*

◀▶ *Salt was vital to prehistoric man; it enabled him to preserve meats by salting them, and to cauterize wounds.*

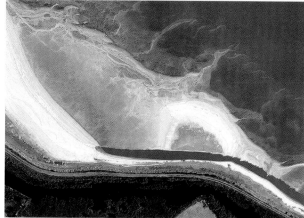

Minerals and the Environment

▲ *Manganese extracted from minerals (shown here, rhodochrosite) has significant antiseptic properties, it is used in water purification.*

▼ *Because of the phosphorus it contains, apatite is a natural soil fertilizer. It is used in the majority of phosphate fertilizers.*

All life on earth, including plants, animals, and humans, depends on precious elements that are contained in rocks. These nourishing substances, which are primarily metals, come to us through the combined action of great forces of nature. The sun, wind, and rain are necessary for a rock to disintegrate and liberate its minerals, which are then transported in the ground by the movement of water. In this way, apatite nourishes the soil with phosphate. The phosphate is absorbed by plants, then by livestock, which eat the plants, and finally by man, who eats the livestock. It is an ecosystem in which minerals are the standards.

Plants and livestock need trace elements to grow and multiply, iron, manganese, zinc, and copper being the main ones. A lack of them in the soil always leads to low production of fodder and meat. This is the reason they are system-atically added to livestock food as in fertilizers. Ancient farmers recognized the value of manure as a fertilizer. They had also noticed the fertilizing action of bones and ashes on the land, without knowing the reason. Since the last century, it has been known that it is due to the presence of three elements indispensable to plant growth: phosphorus, nitrogen, and potassium. These are the basis of artificial fertilizers we use today—phosphates, nitrates, and potassium. Produced at a rate of 150 million tons per year, these fertilizers are responsible for almost half of the world's harvests.

The only shadow on this picture is the very polluting nature of the fertilizer wastes, which threatens to one day disrupt our fragile ecosystem.

▶ *These experimental soils, based on expanded clays of silica or mica, will be used in agriculture in the future.*

▲ *Thallium can be obtained from sphalerite. The metal thallium, like arsenic, can be used as rat poison.*

▲ *The fertility of soils depends on their mineral composition. Here, soils to be used in horticulture: clay, pozzalana, and pebbles.*

▲ *It is possible today to make plants grow without soil. Here, tomatoes grown without soil are planted in rock wool.*

▼ *Hydroponic agriculture permits uninterrupted tomato growing throughout the year.*

▲ *Rose spots, a disease caused by a parasitic mushroom, are treated by spreading sulfur powder on the plant.*

▲ *When they are not planted in soil, tomatoes can receive the necessary trace elements through watering.*

▼ *Phosphates, for which phosphorus is mined (seen here, wavelite) are the most commonly used artificial fertilizers today; however, they are major pollutants.*

◀ *Colemanite. Extracted from colemanite, boron is a soil trace element indispensable for plant growth; it is used as a fertilizer.*

◀ *Rhodochrosite with manganite. Manganese, a trace element for mammals, is found in livestock feed.*

▲ *Fluorite. Today, drinking water is systematically enriched with fluorine for its recognized role in dental hygiene.*

▶ *Chalk, which is traditionally used in agriculture to enhance acid soils, is obtained by burning calcite.*

◀ *Traditionally used as a fungicide, native sulfur is used for the treatment of oidium, a disease caused by a parasitic mushroom on grapevines and roses.*

Healing stone (icosahedron), is highly valued in lithotherapy because its 20 faces promote the concentration of maximum energy on the sick body.

Healing point on a rock crystal. Greek priests placed the rock crystal under the sun to set twigs on fire in order to obtain the sacred fire.

Stones That Heal

The first forms of lithotherapy, stone medicine, revealed a totally magical mentality. Cro-Magnon man's therapy consisted of wearing an amulet for curative properties he ascribed to it because of its shape or color. This was the case with gold, whose sunlike yellow has caused it to be considered a powerful revitalizing agent throughout time. With the help of autosuggestion, this type of treatment perhaps has some chance of healing.

Later, a more rational practice appeared, consisting of rubbing a stone on the sick body. This was based on the discovery of the real properties of certain minerals. Thus it was discovered that when salt was placed in contact with a wound, it could burn and prevent gangrene from setting in—obviously without any knowledge on the part of the healers of the time that it was due to chlorine.

Magnetite, or lodestone, was already used in Greece as a massage stone around 400 B.C. Curiously, this practice regained much favor during the nineteenth century because of the German doctor Franz Mesmer. With magnetism, he claimed to have discovered the means to cure all diseases.

A third method was finally developed, that of reducing the mineral to a powder to ingest as medicine. In the Middle Ages, diamond powder was considered to be an effective antidote to poison, but, composed of pure carbon, it is also very toxic. Pope Clement paid the ultimate price for it in 1534, when, medicated with diamond powder at a price of 40,000 ducats, he gave up his soul to God. Modern medicine is linked to the development of experimental chemistry and is nothing more than the application of this old method of ingestion, but with better control of its undesirable effects.

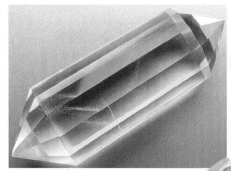

The alchemist doctors of the Middle Ages prepared medications by reducing minerals to powder. Here is a topaz, thought to immunize against poisons.

When Greek doctors saw "superfrozen" water in rock crystals, they advised their patients to put these crystals under their tongues to cool down their bodies.

"Reharmonization" wand. Stone medicine, or lithotherapy, a tradition dating from ancient times, has regained favor among New Age believers.

The Ayurveda, traditional medicine of India, has used the curative properties of minerals for millennia (seen here, massage stones).

Gypsum pillow from China. Chinese doctors prescribe the use of this pillow, perfectly smooth and soft, to ease the nape of the neck and relax the spirit.

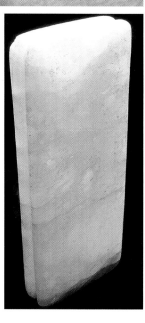

▶ *Modern medicine, based on experimental chemistry, still uses minerals for their therapeutic properties (seen here, fluorine, a source of fluoride).*

▲ *In ancient times, powdered lapis lazuli was used to treat eye diseases and was considered to be a powerful aphrodisiac.*

▲ *Malachite and azurite. In ancient times, wearing malachite was believed to guarantee untroubled sleep.*

◀ *Manganese, a trace element in mammals, is extracted from minerals (seen here, morganite), and is used to feed and to care for livestock.*

▼ *Adularia (moonstone). Moonstone was thought to have revitalizing power, because it was linked to lunar energy by its color.*

▲ *Dolomite is used today to provide magnesium, which is used to treat various medical conditions.*

▲ *Chrysocolla with cuprite. Roman doctors used chrysocolla powder to wash out and treat the eyes, and to disinfect wounds.*

◀ *Calcium can be extracted from calcite. It is a component of numerous medications, especially those used in the treatment of bone diseases.*

Amulets and Talismans

Fluorite from two million years ago found in the prehistoric caves of Le Leisse, in Belgium, were surely amulets, the first protective medallions in history. They were said to work this way: to ward off the ephemeral nature of the world, man has always placed himself under the auspices of a mineral that best symbolizes solidarity, permanence, and eternity to his way of thinking. Involved with the obscure forces that agitate the universe, stone was the medium of divination. The Greeks thought that rock crystal was water that had frozen exceedingly hard on a high mountain, and that it was impossible to make it melt, even in fire. With its exceptional clarity, rock crystal was believed to provide a way to read the future; this is the origin of the crystal balls of our fortune-tellers. An emerald placed under the tongue was also thought to ensure the power of prediction.

Amulets and talismans have no other goal but to attract beneficial forces and keep harmful ones away. In the Orient, turquoise is protection against the evil eye and its powers are even stronger if verses of the Koran are written on it. Blue stones naturally govern the realm of the sky, as is the case of sapphire, the stone of spirituality, or even that of the water, and aquamarine is recommended to people who are taking a long sea voyage.

Red stones, associated with blood, protect during conflicts; a ruby encrusted on the forehead is supposed to make ancient Burmese warriors invulnerable. Yellow stones evoke the sun, and therefore they bring vitality, luck, and love, as does the zircon, the "Venus stone." Green stones, placed under the plant sign, contribute fertility and opulence; thus, the emerald is the guarantee of a happy accumulation of material wealth—you also have to already be rich to be able to afford to buy one.

▲ *Ankh cross in hematite. Because of its blood color, ancient people thought that hematite carried as an amulet would protect a warrior from injury in combat.*

▶ *Triskel, symbol of Celtic energy, placed on labradorite, is traditionally considered to be a protective stone. Amber extracted from the shores of the Baltic Sea were also sacred stones for the Celts.*

▲ *Divining pendulum carved from lapis lazuli. During the sixteenth century, the pendulum was commonly used in Central Europe for mineral prospecting.*

▼ *Protective medallion with an Egyptian motif. The Egyptians wore their jewels on arteries such as the temples, neck, ankles, or wrist in order to conserve the vital fluid that they felt pulsating in these places.*

◀ *Staurolite was thought to have miraculous powers: healing the eyes, curing madness, or calming enraged animals.*

▼ *Staurolite, abundant in the regions of Baud and Coray in Brittany, France, used to be made into rosaries, leading to its name, rosary stone.*

▲ *Chinese protective medallion (pi) in rose quartz. The ancient Chinese venerated rose quartz, often associated with jade, the stone symbol for immortality.*

▶ *Solomon's seal. The sapphire was the sacred stone of the Hebrews. According to the Bible, it was one of the blessings given by God in the Garden of Eden.*

▲ The Russians subjected minerals to scientific experiments to determine their divining usefulness in mineral prospecting.

▶ Pendulum of rock crystal. Formerly, pendulums were used to detect springs and mineral deposits.

Oracle Stone

The word "tourma-line" is from the Singhalese toromalli , "stone that attracts ashes" (left, a black variety, of tourmaline called schorlite). The sorcerers of Ceylon, present-day Sri Lanka, had noticed that, when rubbed, tourmaline attracted light objects; in fact, it emits static electricity. Thus, these sorcerers used the stone to extract oracles from ash patterns left on it.

▲ Divination runes engraved on stones. Whether the rock crystal of the seers, or tourmaline of the sorcerers of Ceylon, stone has always been used as a universal medium of divination.

▼ More than the sorcerer's wand, the crystal pendant is the primary instrument of divining, a detection method based on the natural radiation of the earth.

▲ Here we see untwinned staurolites that are encased in one rock. Some people saw in these shapes the spines on the crown of Christ.

◀ Staurolites often twin, producing unusual shapes. According to an old tradition, they are compared to the shape of the cross.

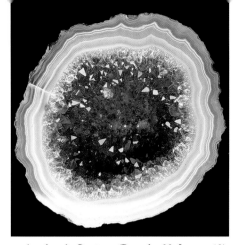

▲ *Amethyst for Capricorn (December 22–January 19), associated with Saturn.*

▶ *About 3,000 years ago, the Chaldeans were the first to assume mysterious links between planets, minerals, and the destiny of men.*

▲ *Jasper for Aquarius (January 20–February 18), associated with Saturn.*

▶ *Sapphire for Pisces (February 19–March 20), associated with Jupiter.*
▼ *Ruby for Aries (March 21–April 19), associated with Mars.*

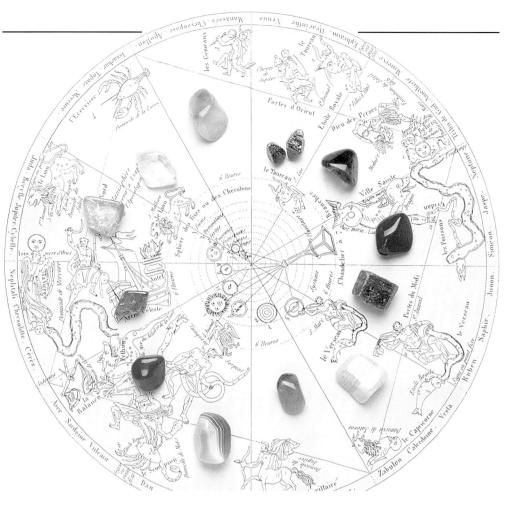

Minerals and Astrology

The custom of associating a stone with a fate goes back more than 3,000 years to the Chaldeans, the first astrologers in history. By observing the sky, they thought they could reveal mysterious connections between the planets, earth minerals, and man. All this took place in the same flow of cosmic energy with which the gods on high pulled the strings. From Mesopotamia, astrology traveled to Egypt, then to Greece and Rome, where the founders of medicine, Hippocrates and Galen, would integrate it into their practice. They believed that health and disease can be largely attributed to the movement of the planets. Each planet regulates a specific part of the human body— the moon for the head, the sun for the heart, Venus for the genital organs, and so on. However, they still attributed a mineral to each planet, which is thought to have a therapeutic effect on the part of the body it controls: Diamonds, associated with the sun, to cure cardiac afflictions; moonstone, associated with the moon, to cure migraines; zircon, yellow, attributed to Venus, to increase sexual activity. In the Middle Ages, astrology enjoyed greater fortune with the development of alchemy. Zodiac stones were carried as lucky charms in amulets. "Birthstones" appeared, "stones of the month," thought to be beneficial for the corresponding time of the year: garnet (January), amethyst (February), aquamarine (March), diamond (April), emerald (May), pearl (June), ruby (July), olivine (August), sapphire (September), opal (October), topaz (November), turquoise (December).

From the seventeenth century on, astrology would be relegated to the ranks of superstition; however, Johannes Kepler established his first mathematical laws governing the movement of the planets, and in so doing, opened the way to modern astronomy.

▲ *Emerald for Taurus (April 20–May 20), associated with Venus.*
▶ *Carnelian for Cancer (June 21–July 22), associated with the moon.*
▼ *Olivine for Leo (July 23–August 22), associated with the sun.*

▲ *Agate for Gemini (May 21–June 20), associated with Mercury.*

▼ *Topaz for Libra (September 23–October 22), associated with Venus.*

▼ *Ruby for Scorpio (October 23–November 22), associated with Mars.*

▲ *Beryl for Virgo (August 23–September 22), associated with Mercury.*
▼ *Sapphire for Sagittarius (Nov. 23–Dec. 21), associated with Jupiter.*

▲ *In Sri Lanka, the star sapphire protects against sorcery. It also contributes purity, wisdom, and fidelity in relationships.*

▶ *Statuettes made of ruby. For the ancient Burmese, ruby was the emblem of warriors. They wore it encrusted in their flesh to make themselves invulnerable.*

▲ *Garnet. A talisman during the Crusades, garnet was a sacred stone throughout the Middle Ages.*

▼ *In Venezuela, the Indians along the Orinoco River always wear amazonite around the neck. They consider it a virtuous stone that protects against bad luck.*

▼ *Water agate, which was so called because of the inclusion of water in its crystal, was formerly credited with the power to create rain.*

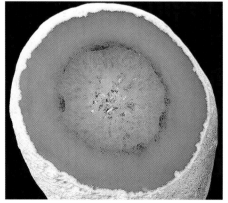

Stones in Legends

There is no prince or conqueror in history who hasn't used stone to consecrate his power—precious stone, of course, perhaps diamond, ruby, sapphire, or emerald. These stones have been traded for at least 7,000 years. Jewels are set in gold and silver on thrones and in royal crowns. Among the Aztecs, turquoise was used for this. It was reserved for the emperor only; anyone else who wore it was condemned to death. The Great Mogol has remained legendary for the Taj Mahal, which he had built in the seventeenth century. No less magnificent is his throne, with its 26,733 gems, including 108 rubies, 116 emeralds, and quantities of diamonds, pearls, and sapphires. Today, it is a national treasure of Iran.

Among other extraordinary stones, the emperor had a diamond weighing 56 grams (280 carats–1.95 oz.), aptly called the Great Mogol. It is thought to have come from a stone weighing 158 grams (5.53 oz.) that the lapidary had destroyed, which is hard to believe when you consider the amazingly high price per carat for an exceptional diamond. The Koh-i-Noor, meaning "mountain of light" was another choice piece, a diamond weighing 37 grams (185 carats–1.30 oz.) that was mined in India 5,000 years previously. The pretenders to the throne of the Great Mogol, Persians, then the Turks, did not hesitate to kill each other for the Koh-i-Noor. As they said, "To possess it is to possess the world." Since 1849 it has belonged to the crown of England, in a slightly reduced size (21 grams–0.735 oz.), having been recut during the reign of Queen Victoria, but it is still the third largest diamond in the world. Queen Elizabeth II wears it as a brooch for rare ceremonies.

▼ *Copper was the third precious metal in ancient times.*

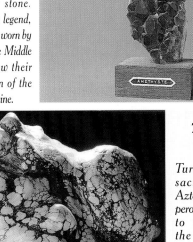

▲ The name amethyst comes from the Greek amethystos, "which protects from drunkenness." Its color implied protection against the effects of wine.

▶ Sobriety stone. According to legend, amethyst was worn by bishops in the Middle Ages to show their renunciation of the pleasures of wine.

Amazonite. Legend has it that the Amazons once lived in the Brazilian forest. To reproduce, they borrowed the services of the Indians, and in exchange, the Indians were given amazonites.

▶ In ancient times, red jasper was worn as an amulet on the thigh to help women give birth and prevent hemorrhages.

The Stone of the Aztecs

Turquoise was the sacred stone of the Aztecs. Only the emperor wore it, attached to his neck, and the piercing of the emperor's nostril was equivalent to the crowning of kings in the West.

In the Orient, it is still the stone that protects from fatal falls; when a person falls, the bezel of the turquoise breaks in his or her place.

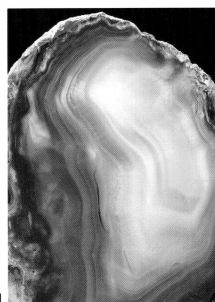

▲ The Romans attributed to malachite the power to protect one from lightning. They recommended it as an amulet to be worn by children.

◀ The Greeks advised jilted lovers to wear an agate because it was thought to make a man attractive to a woman even if she did not like him at first.

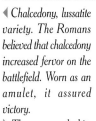

◀ Chalcedony, lussatite variety. The Romans believed that chalcedony increased fervor on the battlefield. Worn as an amulet, it assured victory.

▶ The name malachite comes from the Greek malakhê, "mauve," because of its resemblance to that plant. Consequently, it is considered a fertility stone.

Fossil
Minerals

Azurite, a
copper carbonate,
can mineralize dead organisms but does so less often than
quartz or limestone.

▶ Composed of calcareous skeletons of microscopic marine
animals called foraminifera, chalk can contain curious
inhabitants, such as 50-million-year-old fish.

▲ Pyrite produces stunning fossils whose metallic sparkle
resembles that of gold. For this reason, they are used as
decorative objects.

Petrified Time

Many plant or animal species that have now disappeared are known to us only by their petrified imprints preserved in rocks. These are fossils, of which the oldest (3.8 billion years) take us back to the very origins of life. It all begins with a dead organism sinking into the muddy sediments at the bottom of the water; a volcanic ash is the equivalent environment on land. By covering the organism, the sedimentary coffin will promote the preservation of the body, primarily the hard parts such as the shell, skeleton, teeth, and wood for plants, and the organic tissues will generally decay and the process of fossilization can then begin. This fossilization requires mineral substances that are introduced by the waters in the surrounding sedimentary rock.

This water will either fill in the hollow parts of the organism or permeate the entire organism to chemically transform it into rock; this is the process of epigenesis. Calcium carbonate, silica, and certain phosphates frequently play this role, less often the metallic sulfides such as pyrite, and very exceptionally precious metals such as silver.

Sedimentary rocks, especially clays, sandstone, and limestone, are the principal suppliers of fossils. Fossils are sometimes so abundant that they can make up the entire rock by themselves; this is the case of diatomite, which is formed in a marine environment by the accumulation of siliceous shells of minuscule brown algae called diatoms.

◀ Composed primarily of
quartz and limestone, sandstone is one of the great suppliers
of fossils. Here, a 25-million-year-old
pinecone in a sandstone nodule.

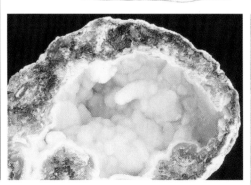

▲ Vivianite becomes encrusted in the bony cavities of dead
animals. Because of this, a perfectly preserved mammoth
cranium was discovered in Mexico.

▲ Chalcedony, which is similar to opal or jasper, replaces dead
organisms with silica, and this naturally creates fine stones.

▲ Silicified araucaria. Silica has replaced the trunk of this
195-million-year-old conifer, preserving its appearance intact.

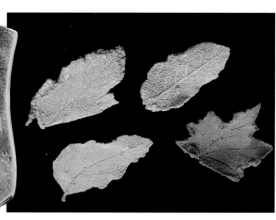

▶ Amber,
a fossil resin from
ancient conifers, some-
times contains small insects.
They are better preserved in amber
than in rock.

▲ A fine layer of limestone is enough to produce imprints of amazing precision by encrustation. Here, oak and ivy leaves.

▼ Fossil wood is transformed into jet by carbonization. The coal reserves of the subsurface are nothing but the fossilized remnants of immense primitive forests.

◀ Coproliths are fossilized excrement of primitive animals, which can be used to reconstruct their diet. In paleontology, the imprint left by the activity of an animal is called a trace.

◀ Trace fossils left in a rock by the passage of primitive worms.

▼ Based on radioactivity, radiochronology makes it possible to date samples of materials from several hundred million years ago (here, with carbon 14).

▲ With fossil species succeeding each other in the layers of the earth according to a rigorous chronology, their presence is a sure method of dating the layers.

▲ Making casts at a site in France where a dinosaur laid its eggs 100 million years ago.

▼ Because of fossils, Buffon was able to write a book on natural history in the eighteenth century, in which the theory of evolution of species had already been postulated.

An Evolving Science

When the Swede Carl von Linné (1707–1779) proposed his species classification system, the organic origin of fossils had just been accepted. Fossils are the most ancient links in the life chain. Up until then, creationist theories considered them to be supernatural creatures, born in the subsurface of the earth. In ancient times, the discovery of fossil remains of dinosaurs fed the myth that there was an ancient race of giants who had preceded man on earth.

▲ Shown here is an impressive fish fossil 55 cm (22 in.) long that was taken from the ground. It is evidence of the presence of an ancient sea on this site, which has now become land.

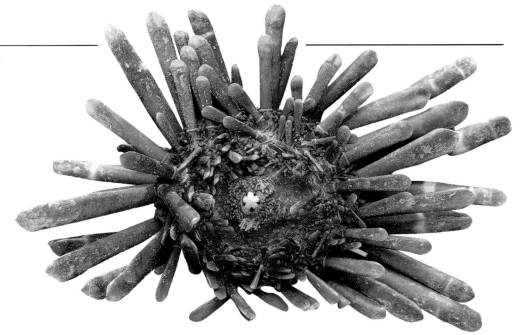

▶ *The present-day sea urchin (Heterocentrotus sp., called "urchin with slate pencils,") is not much different from its fossil ancestors, in spite of 550 million years of evolution.*

▼ *Sea star (Petraster sp.). Echinoderms are among the oldest invertebrates (550 million years); they have given us sea stars, sea lilies, and present-day urchins.*

▲ *Crinoid (Encrinus macrocrinus). This 300-million-year-old echinoderm, extinct today, is related to present-day water lilies.*

▼ *Crinoid (Encrinus liliiformus) dating from 200 million years ago. Crinoids lived attached to the sea bottom by a long stem.*

Our Ancestors, the Sea Urchins

I n the remote past of the Precambrian era, about 3.5 billion years ago, animal life in shallow waters consisted of single-celled microscopic organisms: the amoebae. From this family, the foraminifera evolved, which would later produce chalk through the accumulation of their calcareous shells at the bottom of the oceans. Around 700 million years ago, the first multi-cellular animals appeared, such as the sponges, jellyfish, corals, and annelid worms. All these organisms were still soft and spongy, hardly likely to lend themselves to fossilization; thus primitive worms are known to us only by the trace fossils left by their passage through sediments. The beginning of the Paleozoic era, about 570 million years ago, saw an increase in new animals with bodies now equipped with a solid calcareous framework (echinoderms), sometimes enhanced with a shell (brachiopods and mollusks). Protected from predators by their mineral armor,

they were equipped with powerful arms that allowed them to grab their prey or to burrow in sediments. These new arrivals would become masters of the marine depths.

Limestone has the other virtue of making fossils of these animals more abundant, in such a way that the fossils make it possible to retrace the outline of their evolution. The echinoderms, formidable carnivores, led to a variety of still-existing species, such as the sea lily, sea urchins, sea cucumbers, and sea stars, which are not very different from their ancestors. It is thought that within this family the vertebrate lineage opened up 500 million years ago, leading to man. In spite of their robust calcareous shell, brachiopods have held up less well to the tests of time. Although there are about 7,000 primitive fossil species, barely 260 survive today in the warm waters of the world.

▼ *Fossil of Pentremites sp., which is related to sea lilies. It was known to have lived in warm seas around the world.*

▲ *Brachiopods fossil (Spirifer sp.). First appearing 550 million years ago, the brachiopods are identifiable by their shell, which is made up of two unsymmetrical valves.*

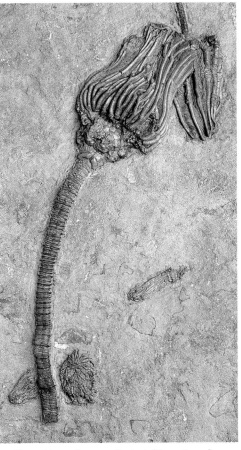

◀ Fossil Actin-ocrinites *sp*. Inside the calyx of this stemmed echinoderm there existed a mouth and ten arms to bring food to its mouth.

▼ Brachiopods fossil. There have been 7,000 fossil species inventoried from the past, compared to 260 today.

◀ Sea urchins (Micro-aster *sp.*) from 100 million years ago. The soft body of the echinoids is covered by a resistant calcareous exterior that is suitable for fossilization.

▼ Sea urchins are known to live buried in marine sediments. When death claims them, they become good candidates for fossilization.

▶ Lichens are the first plants to have left the sea, 470 million years ago. The first terrestrial animals, the arachnids, would soon follow, about 400 million years ago.

▲ Echinoderm fossils (here, urchins) are the subject of intense study. It is thought that within them the vertebrate lineage that led to man opened up.

▼ The oldest fossils are the bacteria, unicellular organisms born on ocean bottoms 3.8 billion years ago, the origin of life.

▲ Sea urchin (Eupatagus *sp.*) from 65 million years ago. Like all echinoids, it had no stem, but rather evolved freely at the bottom of the sea.

Fabulous Ammonites

▲ *Oyster fossil. Mollusks appeared 570 million years ago. Bivalves, including oysters, mussels, and clams, are mollusks.*

▼ *Carnivorous oyster (Rastellum carinatum) from 120 million years ago, with its calcareous shell composed of two symmetrical valves, like all bivalves.*

▼ *Gastropod fossil (Campanile sp). Escargots and slugs came from gastropod mollusks. Some had shells 60 cm (24 in.) long.*

All that remains of primitive mollusks are fossilized shells; nothing remains of the soft organisms in their interior, their eyes, their gills, or their mouths that had serrated teeth. However, we know that they evolved in tropical waters 570 million years ago as the oldest bearers of shells in the animal world. The profusion of forms and dimensions (from 1 mm to 3 m [0.04 in. to 10 ft.] in diameter for the largest shells) reflects the extraordinary diversity that existed in this family. Bivalves—lamellibranches—are the oldest mollusks, the ancestors of present-day mussels, oysters, and clams. In the Middle Ages, their fossils were called "devils' claws" because their shape resembled the hoof of a goat. This animal was considered to be diabolical, like all fossils, which were said to have come back from hell.

Cephalopods, which, like ammonites, are recognizable because of their spiral shell, are the most evolved of the mollusks. Exclusively carnivores, they dominated the seas for hundreds of millions of years, then became rare. Cephalopods are represented by only 400 species today, including cuttlefish, squid, and octopus.

Gastropods are the rare mollusks that left the sea for land, where they became snails and slugs. The ancestor of the snail had a shell 60 cm (24 in.) long. Unfortunately, its speed is unknown.

▶ *Ammonite (Harpoceras sp.) This harpoceras, characteristic of the lower Jurassic period, existed for a short time from 178 to 175 million years ago.*

The Enigma of the Nautiloids

Nautiloids are the first known cephalopods, which were the most evolved group among the mollusks. Their appearance 520 million years ago remains unexplained, because they are not related to any invertebrates that were living at the time. Unlike the ammonites, they survive as the nautilus that exists today in the warm waters of the Pacific.

▲ *Calcified ammonites. Related to cephalopods, ammonites appeared around 395 million years ago, only to disappear inexplicably at the end of the Cretaceous era (65 million years ago).*

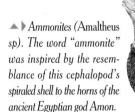

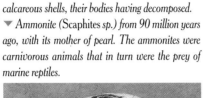

▲ ▶ *Ammonites (Amaltheus sp). The word "ammonite" was inspired by the resemblance of this cephalopod's spiraled shell to the horns of the ancient Egyptian god Amon.*

▲ *Ammonites are known to us only by their calcareous shells, their bodies having decomposed.*
▼ *Ammonite (Scaphites sp.) from 90 million years ago, with its mother of pearl. The ammonites were carnivorous animals that in turn were the prey of marine reptiles.*

▼ *Descendants of the nautiloids, the ammonites are extinct, although they dominated tropical seas for millions of years.*

▲ *Ammonite (Placenticeras sp.) from 70 million years ago. Some ammonite shells are no larger than 3 mm (0.12 in.) but some can reach 3 m (10 ft.) in diameter.*
▼ *Ammonite (Scaphites sp.) from 110 million years ago, fossilized in limestone rock.*

▶ *Fossil of Goniatites sp., this was a cephalopod mollusk that was closely related to the ammonites, which lived about 350 million years ago.*
◀ *Ammonite (Parkinsonia sp.). This was a typically "European" type of cephalopod, from 175 million years ago.*

◀ *Like many mollusks, ammonites produced mother of pearl, a calcareous substance with iridescent reflections that covered the inside surface of their shells.*
▶ *Ammonite (Pictonia sp.). There are only 400 living species of cephalopods today, including the cuttlefish, squid, and octopus.*
◀ *Giant species developed among the mollusks (here is an ammonite), such as Titanosarcolites giganteus, which is 2 m (6 ft.) long.*

▲ *Ammonite (Hildoceras sp.) from 178 million years ago, fossilized in ferruginous limestone.*

Where Do Insects Come From?

▲ *Trilobite (Leonaspis sp.). Appearing in the Cambrian era (570 million years ago), the trilobites are the oldest arthropods, ancestors of insects and crustaceans.*

▼ *Trilobites (Phacops sp.) from 395 million years ago. Marine animals, the trilobites had a chitinous shell divided into three parts, or lobes, thus their name.*

▼ *Trilobite, reconstructed using scattered remains. A few applications of glue were enough to create a very convincing specimen.*

The arthropods make up a particularly large branch within the invertebrates. They include crabs and lobsters, spiders and scorpions, millipedes, and all the known insects, crawling or winged. This is at least 85 percent of the animal species. This whole world originated from small primitive animals called trilobites, which lived in marine waters from 570 to 230 million years ago. This period of time corresponds to almost half of the Paleozoic era, which is therefore called the "era of the trilobites." They undoubtedly descended from segmented worms, the annelids, which are also the source of our garden worms. Trilobites already had all the attributes of the arthropods. They had small "articulated legs," the etymological meaning of the word arthropod, which allowed them to move around on the ocean floor and to scratch in the sediments in search of food. They also had a hard substance, chitin, which held the body entirely within a shell. They shed the shell periodically by molting and this is the origin of their numerous fossils.

Many descendants of the trilobites maintained an aquatic life, such as the crustaceans. Others are, in fact, the first animals to have ventured onto land, 400 million years ago. First came the acarians—primitive spiders—then millipedes, then the collembola, the very first insects. The extraordinary development of the insects—there are more than 1 million species known today—is related to the proliferation of flowering plants beginning about 130 million years ago. From the flowering plants, the insects learned to extract pollen and nectar, and found there an inexhaustible source of food. The chitin of insects, which is not very resistant, is not suitable for fossilization within sedimentary rocks. The best-preserved species are found in amber, petrified resin, which catches insects with their wings deployed as it solidifies. Such fossils are often mounted as jewels.

◀ *Equipped with legs, trilobites were able to move around on the ocean floor, or they burrowed in sediments in search of food.*

▼ *Trilobite (Dalmanites sp.) from 400 million years ago. Primitive arthropods, the trilobites themselves descended from segmented marine worms—the annelids.*

▼ *Trilobite (Cryphaeus sp.). For unknown reasons, the trilobites became extinct at the end of the Paleozoic era, around 230 million years ago.*

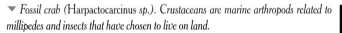

▲ *Fossil crab (Zanthopsis vulgaris) from 25 million years ago.*
Because their shells fill with sediments, the crustaceans have created striking fossils.
▼ *Subantarctic royal crab (Lithodes sp.), present-day species.*

▼ *Fossil crab (Harpactocarcinus sp.). Crustaceans are marine arthropods related to millipedes and insects that have chosen to live on land.*

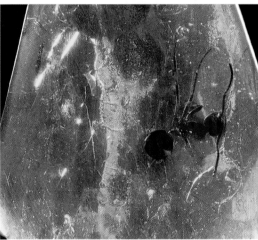

▶ *Red royal crab, a present-day species. With the insects, the crustaceans are the most widespread arthropods. Fossilization is probable because their chitinous integument is highly mineralized.*

▲ *Ant fossilized in amber. Ants appeared only in the Cretaceous era (135 million years ago), well after the first insects, which appeared 395 million years ago.*

▶ *Because they lack hard parts, insects rarely fossilize in rocks. Those preserved in amber are considered precious.*

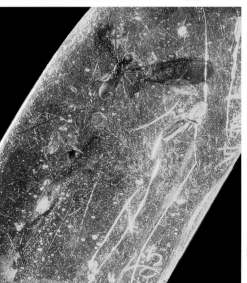

▲ *Fossil of a paleodictopterid. The first winged insects came from this group of primitive hexapods. Insects descended from millipedes and began to diversify in the Carboniferous era.*

Primitive Fish

Fish are the oldest vertebrates. Like us, they have a highly resistant internal skeleton, suitable for fossilization. They have been developing from very primitive forms since 500 million years before our era, through the agnatha, or fish without jaws. The first real representatives date from around 400 million years ago, the cartilaginous fish (chondrichthyes), thus called because their skeleton was not bony. They exist today only as rays and sharks.

In the past, sharks had gigantic proportions. An example is the carcharodon, 20 m (65 ft.) long, which could go down to 3,000 m (9,480 ft.) deep to snap up its prey into its mouth, which was 2 m (6.5 ft.) wide. These sharks are known to us only by their fossil teeth; in the Middle Ages, they were called "Saint Paul tongues," because people considered them to be the serpent tongues that the apostle would have turned into stone, and for this reason they were thought to be powerful against venom.

Bony fish (osteichthyes) appeared later, with a well-ossified skeleton. Evolving first in fresh water, they reached the ocean. Almost all the present-day fish species plus the amphibians, the first vertebrates to put their "flippers" on earth, 370 million years ago, descended from these fish.

▲ *Shark's tooth. Fish with cartilaginous skeletons, the chondrichthyes populated the oceans. Rays and sharks descended from them.*

▼ *Shark's tooth (Carcharodon sp.), 15 million years ago. The tooth measures 13 cm (5 in.). Its mouth could measure 2 m (6.5 ft.).*

▶ *Fossil fish (Vinctifer sp.) from 110 million years ago. It is called a swordfish because of its rostrum resembling that of the present-day swordfish.*

▼ *Fossils of Leptolepis sp. They belong to a group of bony fish, the teleost (from 195 million years ago), from which almost all modern-day fish are descended.*

▲ *Fossil of Furo praelongus. With their bony skeleton, the actinopterygians were better suited to fossilization than the cartilaginous fish.*

▼ *Fossilized jaw of a carnivorous fish (Elleles sp.). The animal lived 110 million years ago and was 2 m (6.5 ft.) long.*

▶ *Osteichthyes fossil (from 110 million years ago). The Osteichthyes are the most evolved of the fish, with an internal bony skeleton and an external skeleton made of scales.*

▶ Fossil of actinopterygian, one of the most primitive forms of bony fish.

▼ Fossil of actinopterygian (*Bourbonella sp.*) from 280 million years ago.

▼ Fish fossil (*Tharias sp.*), seen here in its sedimentary nodule.

▲ Fish in its sedimentary nodule (110 million years old), found in Brazil on the Araripe plateau. Erosion unearthed this nodule.

▶ These nodules were resold by Brazilian peasants, but it is now forbidden to export these nodules.

▲ Fish fossil (*Dapalis sp.*) encased in a limestone slab from the Oligocene era (35 million years ago).

▶ Freshwater fish (*Knightia sp.*) from 40 million years ago, found fossilized in chalk. Bony fish first populated fresh water.

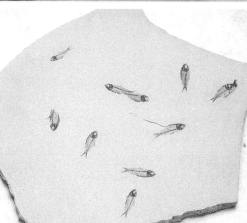

◀ Seen here, the internal ear of a whale. Appearing on earth long after the fish, certain mammals, such as whales, decided to return to the sea.

▼ Fish fossil (*Dapedius pholidotus*). About 500 years of evolution led from the oldest known fish, the agnatha, to the first man.

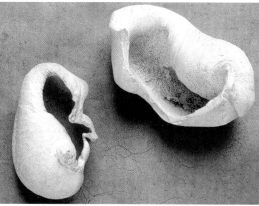

◀ Fish fossil (*Memre sp.*). From fish came the first terrestrial vertebrates, the amphibians, which would eventually lead to man through the reptiles and other mammals.

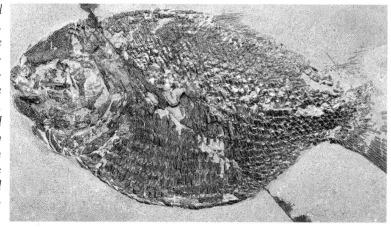

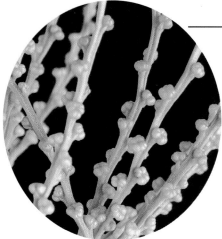

Huge Ferns

▲ *Appearing around 470 million years ago, the first terrestrial plants reproduced by spores, like mushrooms (seen here, a primitive species, still living).*

▶ *Lycopod (Lycopodium grassum). One of the last lycopods still living. Through time, the lycopods have been reduced to grasses.*

▲ *Arborescent lycopodial (Sigillaria brardi). Around 350 million years ago, the arborescent lycopodial appeared, with a trunk sometimes 40 m (130 ft.) high.*

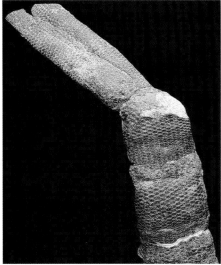

The oldest plants preserved in fossils were bacteria, the unicellular microscopic organisms that evolved at the bottom of the oceans 3.8 million years ago. Because they had no chlorophyll, they did not perform photosynthesis, unlike the algae that appeared in their wake to make up the core of the marine landscape for millions of years. Around 470 million years before our era, an important threshold was crossed when plants liberated themselves from the aquatic environment to migrate to land, followed by the reign of the pteridophytes, very primitive plants that reproduced by spores like lichens. The first forms seen as fossils were the psilophytales, simple stalks with creeping roots and no leaves, from which came the etymology of their name: "naked plants."

Hundreds of millions of years later, the pteridophytes began to develop curious treelike shapes. Then the lycopodiales, the equisetum, and all the first ferns, the filicales, appeared, with trunks occasionally reaching as high as 40 m (130 ft.). Throughout the Carboniferous era, they grew in immense forests; the resulting coal deposits are fossil vestiges of these forests. Through geologic time, the pteridophytes would slowly transform themselves into grasses and disappear for the most part. The lycopodiales exist today only as two herbaceous varieties; of the equisetum, only the little horsetail, 60 cm (23 in.) tall remains. Few ferns have remained treelike.

◀ *The psilophytales were primitive plants that lacked leaves. These plants no longer exist, except for forms of Psilotum nudum.*

◀ *Fossil of Knorria sp., which is related to the arborescent lycopodial. Like them, these plants were part of immense primitive forests.*

▶ *Fossil of Lepidophloios sp., which is related to the arborescent lycopodial.*

▲ *Arborescent horsetail (Annularia sp.) from 300 million years ago. Its trunk had pseudoleaves (microphylls), which brought water to the plant.*

Resurrection Plant

The selaginella (Selaginella lepidophylla) is one of the last living lyco-podials. It is much less imposing in size than its ancestors. In Peru it is known as the resurrection plant because, capable of living without water for years, all curled up, this plant turns green again and reopens instantly when the rains arrive.

◀ *Tree fern (Tietia sp.) The first leaves appeared with the ferns, allowing the plant to breathe and to obtain water.*

▼ *Horsetail (Equisetum hyemale). The arborescent horsetails have survived only as the genus Equisetum, a grass 60 cm (23 in.) in height.*

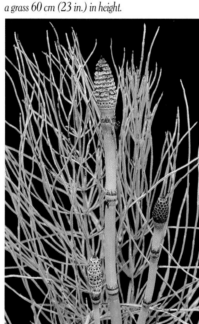

▲ *Trunk of a tree fern (Psaronius augusto-dunensis). Coal deposits are the vestiges of immense fern forests during the Carboniferous era.*

▼ *Arborescent fern (Lygodium sp.) from 40 million years ago. Of the 9,000 species of present-day ferns, very few have remained arborescent.*

▲ *Tree fern (Psaronius bibractensis). Ferns proliferated from 345 to 280 million years ago, reaching gigantic heights.*

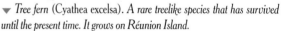

▼ *Tree fern (Cyathea excelsa). A rare treelike species that has survived until the present time. It grows on Réunion Island.*

▲ *Tree fern (Neuropteris gigantea) fossilized in limestone rock from 300 million years ago.*

▶ *Tree fern (Dydimoclaena truncatula.) A present-day species from South America that can reach 6 m (20 ft.) in height.*

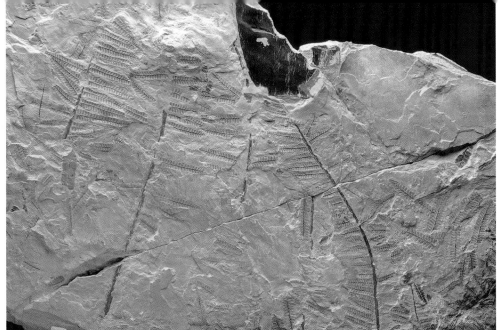

Seed fern (Pecopteris aphalabia). Seed ferns are known to us today only by their fossil forms.

Seed fern (Odontopteris sp.). The gymnosperms were the first plants with seeds, although they don't have flowers or fruit.

Seed fern (Pecopteris arborescens). Appearing about 350 million years ago, seed ferns proliferated throughout the Paleozoic era.

Seed fern (Taenoptieris multinervis).

The Reign of the Flowers

Around 350 million years ago the spermatophytes appeared. These were plants with highly developed reproductive systems, depending on the existence of a seed, which is itself a result of the fertilization of an ovum. Ferns with seeds (pteridosperms) are a remarkable transition between primitive ferns (filicales), which still occupy land, and the higher plants, which succeeded them at the end of the Carboniferous era. At the same time, about 280 million years ago, an unprecedented upheaval caused the breakup of the primitive supercontinent (Pangaea) into two parts: Gondwana in the Southern Hemisphere and Laurasia in the Northern Hemisphere. On Laurasia, which corresponds to present-day Europe, North America, and Asia, the climate would become colder and drier, leading to the appearance of a new population of spermatophytes: the conifers.

Sequoias, araucarias, then pines, firs, spruces, and cedars clustered in immense forests. Their trunks produced resin, which would later fossilize in the ground to create valuable amber. The last qualitative leap of the plant kingdom would occur around 130 million years before our time, with the appearance of the flowering plants (angiosperms). The precious seed was now enclosed in a fruit. Eucalyptus, magnolias, laurels, palms, oaks, chestnuts, grapes, legumes—a multitude of plants appeared, ready to disperse their seeds in conquest of the world; at the beginning of the Tertiary period, 65 million years ago, they already occupied nine-tenths of the plant landscape, essentially the landscape we know today.

Seed fern (Callipteris pellati).

Fossilized trunk of a sequoia.

Seed fern (Colpoxylon aeduense). The cycads are the direct descendants and the last representatives of the seed ferns.

The Petrified Forest

The Petrified Forest in Arizona is one of the great paleontological curiosities. In geologic layers 200 million years old, it is a veritable fossil forest, with trunks that reach as high as 30 m (98 ft.). There is a silicified trunk of a sequoia (1.10 m [3.6 ft.] in diameter). The forest was the second national monument established in the United States, after Mt. Rushmore.

▼ *Silicified araucaria. Araucarias and sequoias are the most representative of the immense primitive forests of the Northern Hemisphere.*

◀ *Silicified araucaria. Arborescent gymnosperms appeared with the conifers, around 295 million years ago.*

▼ *Silicified araucaria still shows traces of the activity of xylophagous worms (longitudinal cut).*

◀ *Silicified araucaria with xylophagous worms (cross-sectional view).*

▼ *Trunk of a walnut. Flowering plants, the angiosperms, appeared 130 million years ago. Since then, the valuable seed has been enclosed in a fruit.*

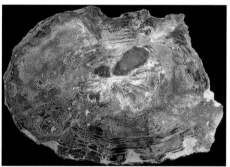

▼ *Eucalyptus leaf (40 million years old). Flowering plants are the most evolved plants, from the eucalyptus to the grapevine through the legumes.*

▲▼ *Pinecone fossil (Araucaria mirabilis), 180 million years old.*

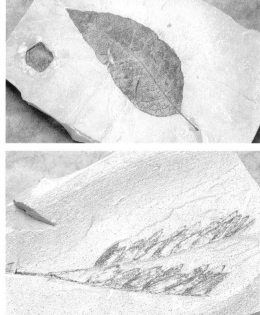

▲ *Maple leaf (40 million years old). The multiplication of the flowering plants promoted the development of animal life.*
◀ *Mimosa leaf. At the beginning of the Tertiary period, 65 million years ago, the flowering plants already made up nine-tenths of the plant landscape.*

The First Steps on Land

▲ *The head of* Actinodon. *Descended from fish, this amphibian lived 280 million years ago in tropical swamps.*
▼ *Bone of* Actinodon. *About 370 million years ago, amphibians were the first terrestrial vertebrates; they were dependent on the aquatic environment, not venturing past the shores.*

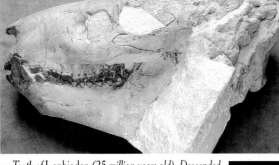

▶ *Dinosaur bone. Around 345 million years ago, the amphibians gave rise to the reptiles. The dinosaurs, which were a reptile population of more than 600 species, later give rise to birds.*

The path that leads from the first terrestrial vertebrates to man is today well marked because of fossils. The amphibians left the sea around 370 million years before our time. Hardly different from their fish ancestors, these ancestors of salamanders still laid their eggs in the water and almost never ventured beyond the banks. Then, 345 million years ago, the amphibians give rise to reptiles. Freed of the aquatic environment, the reptiles laid their eggs on land, like lizards or modern-day snakes. Very mobile, they became masters of the planet during the Mesozoic era, which is called "the age of reptiles" for this reason.

The real masters are the dinosaurs, a reptilian population spread out among 600 species. The smallest, *Compsognathus*, was the size of a chicken, and the largest, *Brachiosaurus*, could swallow a refrigerator in a single gulp. The name dinosaur, which etymologically means "terrible saurian," was only partially justified. Although *Tyrannosaurus rex* was a voracious carnivore, *Diplodocus* looks like a placid herbivore, although 35 m (115 ft.) long. One group would try to fly, giving rise to birds around 150 million years ago. This is the *Archeopteryx*, a winged dinosaur the size of a crow, discovered in 1961 in the quarries at Sohnhofen (Germany).

For reasons that are still not clear, the dinosaurs abruptly disappeared about 65 million years ago, perhaps the victims of a meteor impact. They give way to a class of vertebrates, the mammals, sprung from reptiles around 200 million years ago. Their name comes from the fact that they feed their young with mammary glands. Although some have chosen to return to the sea (whales), or to fly (bats), the majority stay on land, producing a steady stream of species increasingly better armed to occupy the territory. Thus was born man, who appeared around 4.5 million years ago in a still very rough form: *Australopithecus*.

▶ *Mammoth molar from 100,000 years ago. Mammoths appeared at the same time as Neanderthal man, another mammal.*
◀ *Head of a primitive sheep (*Merycoidodon sp.*) from 25 million years ago. This mammal is an ancestor of our present-day ruminants but its teeth reveal carnivorous characteristics.*

▼ *Tooth of* Lophiodon *(25 million years old). Descended from reptiles, mammals appeared around 200 million years ago. Here, a primitive tapir the size of a rhinoceros.*

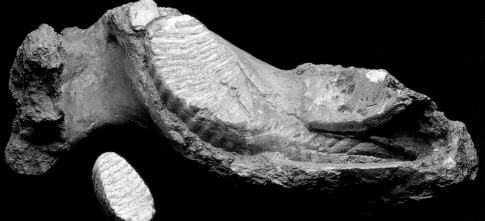

▲ *Mammoth mandible. The perfectly preserved ivory from the mammoths fossilized in the Siberian ice has been the subject of significant trading for many years. The thawed meat was given to dogs to eat.*

▼ *Baby lynx. After the extinction of the dinosaurs 65 million years ago, mammals came to dominate the earth.*

▲ *Glyptodon (4 m [13 ft.] in length), relative of the present-day armadillos. In what is now America, where they lived until about 15,000 years ago, they are mentioned in Indian legends.*
◀ *This "sea cow" (Rhytina gigas) 8 m (26 ft.) in length, lived in the Pacific Ocean. Hunted by fishermen for its meat, it disappeared in 1863.*

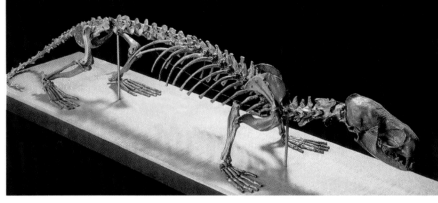

▲ *A primitive otter (Potamotherium valetoni) from 30 million years ago. Many mammals, like the otter, kept the aquatic activity of their marine origins.*

▲ *Mammal from the Quaternary period with reddish fleece and great curved tusks.*
▼ *The large vertebrates are a favorite attraction of visitors to museums of natural history throughout the world (here, the museum in Nantes, France).*

A 140-Million-Year-Old Crocodile

Crocodileimus robustus, *a reptile similar to the present-day crocodile, lived 140 million years ago. It is known to us by its 56 cm (22 in.) fossil, wonderfully preserved, discovered in the limestone of Cerin, France. Related to the dinosaurs, crocodiles are the only group of primitive reptiles, or archosaurians, to have survived to this day.*

Collectors' Minerals

▲ *Rocks are essentially homogenous masses of minerals. They make up the external part of the earth.*
▼ *Most rocks are hard, but some, like sand, as seen here, are movable.*

▲ *Limestone rocks on the shore of the Aegean Sea. Sedimentary rocks are made up of rock debris, or sediments, which slowly become cemented together.*
▼ *In Burren, Ireland, an exceptional flora succeeds in growing in the rocky interstices; it resembles species that are both tropical and polar.*

▲ *Rocks generally contain several minerals, but marble and quartzite have only one—marble has calcite and quartzite has quartz.*

From Minerals to Rocks

Rocks make up the surface material of the earth's crust, the familiar soil we live on. Rocks are generally made up of several minerals, but some, such as marble and quartzite, contain only one mineral. Contrary to the popular notion, rocks are not always hard. They can be movable (sand), plastic (clay), liquid (petroleum), and gaseous (natural gas). Three large rock families can be distinguished, according to the conditions that prevailed when they were formed: magmatic, sedimentary, and metamorphic. As their name indicates, the magmatic rocks were produced by the cooling of magma, the melted fluid of mineral matter that bubbles up into the depths of the earth at 1,200°C–2,192°F and that sometimes flows forth on the earth as lava. In some cases, such as with plutonic rocks, the solidification of the magma has occurred at depth (up to 50 km [31 mi.]), through stages of cooling that are so slow that the rock has time to crystallize well. This is the case with granite, with its well-defined crystals of quartz, feldspar, and mica, which may reach several centimeters (1 cm = 0.4 in.) in size (phenocrysts). In other cases, such as with volcanic rocks, the cooling took place near the surface, so rapidly that the rock was able to develop only microcrystals (basalt). The rock can also be found as a vitrified solid, which had been melted into an undifferentiated mineral substance. This is the case with obsidian, a volcanic glass.

Sedimentary rocks are made up of fine rocky particles that have been deposited on the ocean floor—or any natural trough on land—and are progressively cemented. The well-consolidated debris are microscopic (argillites), or about 1 mm (0.04 in.) in size, such as sandstone, or even large pebbles, such as conglomerate.

Metamorphic rocks are magmatic or sedimentary rocks that have undergone a transformation of their texture due to heating or ambient pressure. The minerals that make up metamorphic rocks have been transformed. Marble, recrystallized limestone, and quartzite, metamorphosed sandstone, fall into this category.

▲ *Burren, in Ireland, called "the Giants' Causeway." In the course of millennia, erosion has leveled the limestone rock, and it has become smooth.*
▶ *The Isle of Tenerife (Canary Islands). Erosion cuts into the mass of rock, here leaving only this rocky needle (in the background, Teide Peak).*

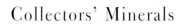

▼ *Magma bubbling at 1,200°C (2,192°F) within the earth sometimes escapes as lava. Here, a solidified lava flow in the Galapagos Islands.*

▲ *Granitic cliffs of Half Dome in Yosemite (California). Granite is a magmatic rock that is created by the cooling of magma at depth (50 km [31 mi.]).*

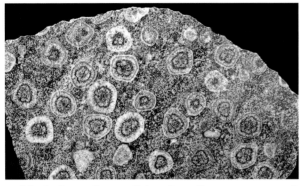

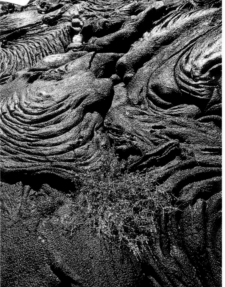

▲ *Orbicular diorite in Corsica, called napoleonite. Diorite is a magmatic rock similar to granite in its granular texture, but darker in color.*

▶ *Created by volcanism, the Galapagos Islands harbor stunning flora and fauna (iguanas, giant tortoises) that Charles Darwin studied during his voyage on the American continent.*

▲ *Pegmatite with black amphibole. Pegmatites are granite that contain very large crystals (or phenocrysts) of quartz, feldspar, and mica.*

▼ *Pumice, or pumice stone, is a porous rock of volcanic origin. Very light, capable of scratching steel, it is used as an abrasive.*

▲ *Vesuvianite (idocrase) on quartzite, a metamorphic sandstone whose sand grains have been welded together under pressure.*

▲ *Volcanic bombs are projectiles of liquid magma that are expelled by volcanoes. The magma solidifies afterwards. It is not unusual to find olivine in them.*

▶ *Jet that is used in jewelry and other objects is a variety of coal, a fossil rock resulting from the decomposition of old plants.*

◀ *Rock with mica and garnet. The study of rocks is called petrography. This is not to be confused with mineralogy, which is the study of minerals, the building blocks of rocks.*

▲ *Siderite with quartz and wolframite. Siderite, a carbonate made up of two-thirds iron, is thus an important iron ore.*

▼ *Cerussite with barite. Cerussite is a lead carbonate. It is formed by the contact of carbonic acid and lead. Almost 200 minerals are carbonates.*

Mineral Chemistry

Similar to a giant erector set, the mineral universe is based on a small number of elements, 109 of them. Some of the elements are gases, such as oxygen, for example, but most of the others are solid. Some are found isolated underground; these are called native elements. They include all the metals and some nonmetallic elements such as arsenic, sulfur, and carbon—pure carbon is diamond. Combined with oxygen or with hydrogen, they produce many other minerals.

The oxides and hydroxides are a group of 520 minerals. The hydroxides are metals that have corroded in contact with oxygen or hydrogen, as in the classic case of rust, which is an iron hydroxide. The sulfides make up a group of 540 minerals. As their name suggests, they are composed of sulfur and metals; for example, lead is present in galena as lead sulfide; zinc is found in sphalerite as zinc sulfide.

The halide group of 150 minerals links a metal to a halogen such as fluorine, chlorine, bromine, iodine, or astatine. The most common halide is salt, a compound of chlorine and sodium. Its old Greek name of *halos* was used as a name for minerals of this group because, like salt, halides were often soluble in water and had a tangy taste.

In chemistry an acid is a natural compound of oxygen, hydrogen, and a third element that may be sulfur, carbon, phosphorus, and so on. When it comes in contact with a metal, the acid has a tendency to get rid of its hydrogen in order to have metal take its place, which then becomes a new solid called a "salt." This action, which is very common in nature, is the origin of many mineral groups, of which there are about 200 carbonates, (salts of carbonic acid), 270 sulfates (salts of sulfuric acid), 390 phosphates (salts of phosphoric acid), and others. Silicates result from the many chemical combinations of silicon, the most widespread element in nature after oxygen. This gigantic group of 916 minerals alone makes up 95 percent of the earth's crust, by weight.

▲ *Anhydrite, which is similar to gypsum, is a calcium sulfate, a natural salt of sulfuric acid. Adding anhydrite to water creates gypsum.*

◀ *Hubnerite with quartz. Hubnerite, which is a manganese tungstate, is a tungstic acid salt valued for its 75 percent tungsten content.*

◀ *Crocoite is a lead chromate, a salt of chromic acid. This rare mineral is found in veins when lead is altered by chromium.*

◀ *Wulfenite is a lead molybdate, a salt of molybdic acid. It was described in 1785 by the mineralogist Xavier Wulfen, from whom it received its name.*

▶ *Coating of white quartz. Quartz is an oxide of silica, a compound of the two most common elements in nature: oxygen and silicon.*

◀ 101 native elements, chemically uncombined, are found isolated in the subsurface. Some are metals and their natural alloys (here, nickel).
▼ Like arsenic and antimony, bismuth is a metalloid, a native element with properties similar to metals, but not malleable.

▲ Sulfides are a group of 540 minerals, including ores. Here, we see galena, a lead sulfide.
▼ Pyromorphite with wulfenite. Pyromorphite is a lead chlorophosphate that is formed by the alteration of lead on contact with phosphoric acid.

▼ Fluorine, a compound of fluorine and calcium, or calcium fluoride. Like salt, it belongs to the halide group (150 minerals).

▶ Roselite is an arsenate, a salt from arsenic acid that is colored pink by the presence of cobalt. The best specimens of this rare mineral come from Morocco.

▼ Chemical combinations of silica produce silicates (here, we see axinite), a family of 916 metals, making up 95 percent of the earth's crust by weight.

◀ Endlichite contains arsenic in its formula. In this respect, it differs from vanadinite, the most common of the vanadates or salts from vanidic acid.
▶ Vivianite is a hydrated iron phosphate. It belongs to the group of 390 phosphates, to which arsenates and vanadates are traditionally added.

◀ Iron-bearing gypsum sword. By growing close together, two crystals can become fused and develop symmetrically; seen here, so-called "Siamese twins."

▶ Japanese twin (or Gardette twin), characteristic of quartz. Almost 700 minerals can twin, either by simple contact or by interpenetration.

▲ The geometric shapes formed by twinning are constant and often characteristic of the mineral; seen here, twinned "dovetail" gypsum.

Crystal Shapes

Cubes, rhombuses, and perfect triangles that appear to have been perfectly lined up. Obviously, geometry is at the heart of a crystal. And this is not merely an image; it is already there in the crystal lattice, this microscopic germ of matter corresponding to the most elementary form of a crystal in the process of being made. In the interior, the atoms are organized according to rigorous symmetry, something not found in gases or liquids, which are thus called "amorphous."

The Frenchman René Just Haüy discovered this phenomenon in 1784 when he accidentally broke calcite. He saw that the scattered pieces, from the smallest to the largest, had the same shape as the original crystal, which was a parallelepiped with rhombic faces. He concluded from this that calcite was an overlapping of an infinity of lattices with identical structures, which started from an original parallelepiped, and had constructed a larger and larger network until the crystal was complete. He discovered six other primitive solids or crystal systems, which, from the cube to the prism, are the basis of all existing mineral shapes. In truth, these original shapes are rarely found in nature.

In the process of growth, many accidents can occur that undermine the structure and make it deviate from its construction into impure forms. Innumerable crystal designs result, including acicular, leaf, hair, or fibrous forms. Only a trained eye can determine the original crystal structure. An isolated crystal is a rare thing in nature. More often, crystals occur with others, in contact or by interpenetration. When this happens in an organized way, twins result, which are combinations of two, or even three or four, crystals. Some are very characteristic of the mineral, such as the cross-shaped twinning of staurolite or the calcite butterfly. Beyond four crystals, the association becomes more uncertain and even downright messy. Then there are aggregates, botryoidal, mamellar, fan-shaped, dendritic, and so on.

◀ Interpenetration of two quartz crystals in the shape of a cross.

▲ Twinned fluorite. The simple twin is formed by two crystals. There can be three or four crystals (triplets and quadruplets).

▲ Elbow twin, characteristic of cassiterite. Less commonly, rutile also produces elbow twins.

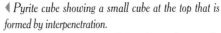

◀ *Pyrite cube showing a small cube at the top that is formed by interpenetration.*
▼ *Garnet often occurs as well-formed crystals, generally (as shown here) as dodecahedra, twelve-sided crystals (or trapezohedra).*

▶ *Interpenetration of two pyrite crystals.*

▲ *Pyrite is made up of an overlapping infinity of cubes, from the primitive lattice up to the final crystal.*
▼ *Pyrite octahedron on hematite. Pyrite can occur as an octahedron (eight faces), which is very characteristic; for this reason, it is called pyritohedron.*

Mineral Transformation

When subjected to particular conditions of alteration, a mineral can be chemically transformed into another mineral. The internal structure will be modified, but not the initial shape, which persists; this is called pseudomorphism. Here, a quartz pseudomorph after anhydrite, where quartz has taken the place of anhydrite, without affecting the crystalline shape.

▶ *Here we see giant garnet crystal in rock. When nothing hinders its growth, minerals develop perfect geometric shapes.*

▼ *Erythrite often occurs as compact crusts in cavities or as so-called pincushions that can reach 10 cm (4 in.) in length.*

▲ *If nothing disturbs its growth, magnetite occurs naturally as well-formed octahedra; otherwise it is found as a mass, with indistinguishable crystals.*

▶ *Disordered groups of several crystals are called aggregates. Here, a mass of garnets arranged with no particular symmetry.*

The pink of kammererite is due to the chromium it contains.

Mineral Colors

▲ *Kyanite (or disthene) is generally blue; its name is taken from the Greek kuanos, "dark blue."*

▲ *Color is not the best criterion for the identification of a mineral. Fluorite, for example, can be yellow, violet, blue, green, pink, brown, black, and even colorless.*

▲ *The copper contained in malachite is the reason for its deep green color. Copper also causes the blue in azurite, a mineral often associated with malachite.*

▼ *Green fluorite is carved by Chinese artisans under the name of green quartz, but its hardness of 4 cannot begin to compare with that of quartz (7).*

The color of a mineral is the first thing that catches the eye, but be careful—color is far from being the best criterion for identification. The difference between the blue of lazurite and that of lazulite is very slight, but it is much more than the single letter difference in their names. It is only in testing their reactions to a flame that it can be determined that the color of one is due to sodium, and that of the other to magnesium; they have nothing to do with each other. In a ruby, several atoms of chromium have slipped into an aluminum compound to give it its red color; the same element, chromium, in contact with beryllium and aluminum, produces the green color of the emerald.

The mineral color chart is subtle. It shows an atomic kitchen where the basic ingredients are known to us, but the binding agents that make the recipe succeed are not always known; a color theory has yet to be invented. Right now we are at the stage of describing the phenomena, which is already complex. When the color of a mineral is due to its chemical composition, it is said to be idiochromatic. It contains a preponderant element in its formula, which tends to leave its signature color to minerals that it enters into: black minerals for iron, red for manganese, yellow for uranium. No general principle can be stated, because copper also gives red to cuprite and green to malachite and blue to azurite. Other minerals owe their colors to impurities that are introduced into their crystals (allochromatic color), whereas by their chemical composition they are naturally colorless. This is the case of hyaline quartz, clear as spring water is pure, but fine inclusions of mica are enough to color it green; with manganese, it becomes pink. In the third case, color is caused by the crystal being in contact with light (pseudochromatic color). The light modifies the color of the mineral as long as the mineral remains exposed to the light source, hence the opal or labradorite, whose iridescence is purely an optical effect.

▲ *Rutile included in this crystal has colored the quartz red; without rutile, quartz is naturally colorless, an example of allochromatic color.*

▲ *Quartz with green inclusions of chlorite, which have not colored the crystal.*
▶ *Quartz crystal containing fine orange inclusions of rutile.*

▼ The iridescence of labradorite is caused by the reflection of light on its crystal. It is a purely optical effect of pseudo-chromatic color.

▼ Generally colorless or white, calcite can also be colored, but always pale colors (shown here, orange), due to impurities in its crystal.

▲ Moonstones or opals stand out, like labradorites, because of their pseudochromatic color.

▼ Some transparent varieties of calcite are used as lenses in microscopes. The yellow-green variety, seen below, has only decorative value.

▲ Violet and yellow ametrine is a natural mixture of amethyst and citrine, from which it gets its name. Its appearance on the gem market is recent, less than 30 years.

▼ Yellow-orange imperial topaz (below) and pink topaz are varieties of this very diversely colored gem that is in great demand for jewelry.

▲ Charoite is a silicate that is present in the composition of a beautiful blue rock traditionally used in Siberia for carving vases.

▶ Rich in zinc, sphalerite is generally honey yellow, brown, or black, according to the iron or manganese impurities it contains. It is rarely colorless.

◀ Ametrine quartz with white flecks in its crystal. These flecks can embellish a stone, as in the case of emerald, where the flecks are called "garden."

Transparency and Luster

A pure quartz crystal is naturally transparent and colorless. Light travels through it unobstructed. This is the zero degree of mineral purity, which is also attained by topaz, beryl, and diamond. People in ancient times found this optical property so fascinating that they attributed all sorts of magical virtues to it. The Greeks "saw" the future in the clearness of quartz. Using it as a lens under the sun, they marveled at its power to light twigs, thus obtaining their "sacred fire." From beryl, they learned to manufacture eyeglasses, that were still called "beryls" in the Middle Ages.

Today, transparency no longer holds so much importance for us, but it is still necessary that a precious stone dazzle those who see it with all its fire. This can be rather delicate, because the introduction of a foreign substance into the crystal, even in an infinitesimal amount, can cause the crystal to become cloudy. It becomes translucent; the light still passes through it, but now we can't see through it and it becomes less pleasing when cut. These inclusions in the crystal are often solids, sometimes water bubbles or gas. Almost always, they cause coloration. Some of them are extremely beautiful, such as rutile needles in quartz, called Venus hair or love arrows.

Many minerals are naturally opaque; neither light nor vision pass through them. Unusable as gems, they still have value, such as gold, for starters. The luster of a mineral is the brilliance it reflects when light shines on it. It has more to do with its texture or the grain of the stone. Metallic luster is characteristic of all metals and some sulfides; the other minerals have nonmetallic luster. Nonmetallic luster ranges from vitreous to adamantine for the most brilliant, and from greasy to resinous, silky, pearly, waxy, or earthy for the duller minerals.

◀ Golden Venus hair quartz. Fine inclusions of rutile in quartz cause the Venus hair, which is also referred to as "love arrows."

▶ Quartz with inclusions of rutile and mica. Inclusions are impurities that are incorporated into the crystal during its growth.

▼ Although it is a rare phenomenon, garnets occur as inclusions in this quartz crystal.

◀ Quartz crystal with inclusions of rutile. Inside, the "negative crystal" can be seen, a void in the quartz where its crystalline form was reproduced.

▶ Quartz crystal with inclusions of rutile and ankerite. Inclusions are often solid, but can also be liquid or gaseous.

▲ *Quartz with fine argillaceous inclusions. When inclusions color a crystal, often making it translucent, they are called "chromophores."*

▼ *Quartz crystal with inclusions of chlorite and dolomite.*

▶ *A translucent mineral (seen here, tourmaline) lets light filter through; however, it is impossible to see through it. Such a crystal cannot be faceted.*

◀ *Rock crystal quartz is naturally transparent; light travels through it unimpeded, and it is possible to see through it. Transparency is a valuable quality in a gem.*

▼ *An opaque mineral (seen here, marcasite) does not allow light or vision to pass through it. Any opaque mineral is by definition unsuitable as a gem.*

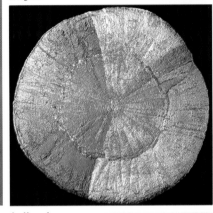

▶ *This fluorite has become translucent due to several phases of crystal growth, which can be clearly seen here.*

▼ *Galena, like many sulfides, such as boulangerite, bournonite, marcasite, stibnite, and so on, have metallic luster similar to that of metals. Unlike elemental metals, however, these are chemical compounds.*

◀ *Apophyllite has vitreous luster similar to that of glass. It is characteristic of many silicates that are rich in silica, such as quartz.*

▼ *Metallic luster that is characteristic of metals (below we see copper) is distinguished from nonmetallic luster of other minerals. Metallic luster is distinguished from others by its higher reflective capacity.*

▼ *Dolomite has pearly luster reminiscent of the mother of pearl of shells. This luster is due to the scaly nature of the mineral.*

▲ *Aragonite is breakable; it is known to crumble when it is cut.*

▶ *Stibnite is sectile; it can be cut with a knife.*

▼ *Boulangerite is flexible; although it is known to bend without breaking, it does not revert to its original shape.*

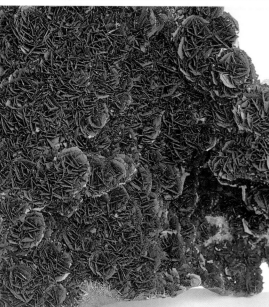

▲ *Hematite is elastic; it reverts to its original form after being bent.*

Hard as a Rock?

Hardness is an important method of identifying minerals, generally much less misleading than the simple examination for shape or color. Hardness is resistance to scratching. Some solids are so soft that a fingernail will scratch them; other minerals need a knife or steel file or something harder to scratch them.

The Austrian mineralogist Friedrich Mohs established a hardness scale (called the Mohs scale) in 1822, in which he ranked 10 representative samples on a scale from 1 to 10. It is a relative measurement, meaning that a mineral that is categorized on a higher level is capable of scratching a mineral below it. Talc is ranked at 1; this is the softest of all minerals, which is the reason its powder has long been used for care of the skin. Starting with the rank of 3, a mineral cannot be scratched with a fingernail. From 5 on, a knife blade can glide across a crystal without damaging it. From 8 on, the mineral is too hard to be scratched by glass. At the top of the scale is diamond, the hardest of the minerals, 140,000 times more abrasive than talc. Diamond is so hard that it cannot even be scratched by itself, which is why its powder is traditionally used to polish precious stones.

Tenacity is a different concept; it is the resistance of the mineral to cutting. Some minerals are sectile, malleable, ductile, plastic, flexible, or elastic. Although diamond is very hard, it has very low tenacity, shattering like glass if one tries to break it. Other much less majestic minerals, such as gypsum or hematite, will bend without breaking, like a blade of grass.

▼ *Greeks and Romans created cameos with unequaled mastery. Their favorite materials were onyx, agate, or malachite.*

◀ *Copper, like all metals, is both ductile and malleable.*

▶ *Engraving on stone or glyptics requires minerals that are hard enough to be carved in relief—this is the art of the cameo.*

▼ *Hardness of 3: calcite. Marble is considered one of the best rocks to carve because it has the low hardness of calcite, its principal constituent.*

▲ *Hardness of 1: talc, 140,000 times softer than diamond. Today it is used as powder for skin care.*

▶ *Hardness of 2: gypsum. Like talc, gypsum can be scratched by a fingernail. The Etruscans carved bas-reliefs out of gypsum for their tombs.*

◀ *Hardness of 5: apatite. Its hardness is such that a knife blade is necessary to scratch it.*

▲ *Hardness of 4: fluorite. Fluorite was carved by the Romans, who used it to make drinking vessels, the Murrhin vases that became famous.*

◀ *Hardness of 6: orthoclase. This stone is used in jewelry, especially the moonstone variety.*

◀ *Hardness of 8: topaz. At this degree of hardness, the mineral begins to have the ability to scratch glass.*

▲ *Hardness of 7: quartz. This is the ideal hardness for faceting a stone, provided it is transparent.*

◀ *Hardness of 9: ruby. Like all corundums, ruby, a non-gem, is used as an abrasive in industry.*

▶ *Hardness of 10: diamond. This hardest of the minerals cannot even be scratched by itself. To cut and polish it, one must resort to using diamond powder.*

Beginning Your Collection

▲ *Label your samples well; the term chlorite is imprecise for this kammererite, one of the chromium-bearing varieties of the chlorite group.*

▼ *There are 3,500 named minerals, but more than 10,000 varieties. The feldspars (shown here, with mica) make up a particularly diverse mineral group.*

If reading this book has awakened a vocation in you and you want to become a mineral collector, read on. First of all, you need to know you will never be able to collect all 3,500 minerals found in nature—this number goes up to 10,000 if all the varieties are counted. Although 300 are the most common, all the others are rare and thus expensive; a beautiful pink fluorine may cost as much as a precious stone. And the majority of minerals can be seen only under a microscope. The choice for a collection then becomes that of a theme: a mineral family or minerals from the same region.

If you choose to take off across land, the use of geologic maps will give you information about the mineralogic nature of a site and about the most fertile areas for discovery, but be careful—pits, quarries, and abandoned mines are tempting for the collector, but these places are dangerous and access to them is forbidden. Don't turn your hobby into a painful survival exercise. Going to mineral shows is more relaxing and an equally effective way of enriching your collection.

Once the samples are in your home, several instruments will prove useful for identifying them: a binocular microscope, hardness pencils, a torch for possible flame tests. Don't forget to label your minerals well, especially where they come from. Then there is the problem of space. Crystals tens of centimeters (4 in. and larger) in size are common currency in nature, but these are not the ones you ought to collect, or you may see your house turned into megalithic bric-a-brac. A mineral specimen 10 cm (4 in.) in size is about the maximum. Some minerals are difficult to keep in a collection because they change under light (fluorite, proustite) or oxidize; marcasite, containing sulfuric acid, threatens to damage minerals placed near it. Not to mention the radioactive minerals (pitchblende, autunite) that should be kept 2 m (6.5 feet) away, or simply avoided.

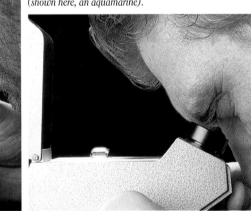

◀ *For informed mineralogists, the spectroscope shows the spectrum of the mineral, the way the crystal decomposes light (shown here, an aquamarine).*

▼ *The binocular scope (here, at a magnification of 10) is indispensable to the collector. This scope is like a microscope, as the majority of minerals are invisible to the naked eye.*

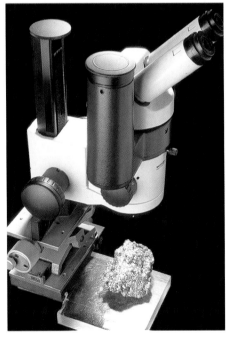

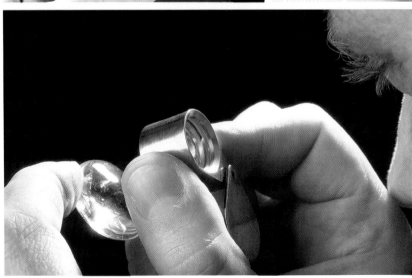

▲ *The refractometer allows the measurement of the mineral's indices of refraction (shown here, an amethyst). This is an indispensable instrument in gemology.*

◀ *The hand lens is the instrument that collectors should keep with them at all times, whether in the field or at mineral shows.*

▲ *Alabaster is one of the massive varieties of jasper.*

▲ *Selenite is a fibrous variety of gypsum. Its name, from the Greek selênê (moon), comes from its characteristic pearly luster.*

▼ *Minyulite. This is a phosphate that is highly valued by collectors.*

▲ *"Iron eye yellow" is a variety of jasper that is very much valued as a decorative stone.*

▼ *Wulfenite, previous called "yellow lead ore," is a highly valued mineral, although it changes easily in a collection.*

▲ *Blue jasper from Brazil.*

▼ *Mimetite can easily fool the amateur collector, because it resembles both pyromorphite and vanadinite.*

▼ *Brought back from South Africa in the eighteenth century by the Dutchman van Prehn, prehnite is a beautiful collectors' mineral whose appearance is similar to jade.*

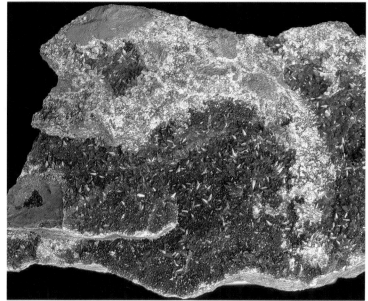

▲ *Andalusite. Discovered in Andalusia, this aluminum mineral is highly prized for the rare transparent varieties from Sri Lanka and Brazil.*

▼ *A mineral of iron and manganese that is rare in nature, purpurite is prized for its deep purple color verging on violet, which is also the source of its name.*

Rare Stones, Collectors' Treasures

Interest in mineralogy in the eighteenth century led to the creation of the exhibition rooms for natural history, places where, for the first time, minerals were rigorously classified and their scientific study was begun. They became the foundations of the great national collections that we can visit today. One day would not be enough to review the approximately 150,000 minerals that are on display, presented in the classical way as a collection in display cases.

The British Museum in London, created in 1753, possesses the largest mineral collection in the world, the result of its long history of activity in the earth sciences. This history includes the founders of modern geology, such as William Smith (1769–1839) or Charles Lyell (1797–1875). The National Museum of Natural History in Paris, which dates back to 1635, is also a high point of scientific mineralogy. Here, the clergyman Haüy (1743–1822) established the basics of crystallography, the study of crystal properties, with applications that are still being used in the field of electronics. The collections of the Museums of Natural History in Vienna, Prague, St. Petersburg, and the one in the Mineralogic Institute of Freiberg, Germany, are also obligatory stops.

In the United States, the Smithsonian Institution in Washington, D.C., is the place to visit because of the famous and important pieces that can be seen there. One is the Hope diamond, the famous blue diamond that, it is said, will bring death and misery to those who possess it. With about one million private collections, the mineral passion has reached a peak in the United States. Two stunning types of minicollections have developed here, such as the "thumbnail" collection with its samples 2.5 cm (1 in.) in size, and "micromounts," about a millimeter, observable only under a microscope.

▲ *Like rutile and brookite, anatase is an important titanium mineral. Too rare to be used as ore, it is of special interest to collectors.*

▼ *Axinite, a collectors' mineral highly prized for its crystals with cutting edges that give it its name, from the Greek axis, "axe."*

▲ *When it oxidizes, marcasite liberates sulfuric acid that attacks display cases and minerals placed near it. It is a scourge for collectors.*

▲ *Crocoite. Its saffron color gave it its name, from the Greek krokos, which means saffron. It is a rare mineral, mined in Tasmania and all over Austria.*

◀ *Dioptase, a silica, lends itself well to cutting and was for a long time considered a variety of emerald. It is one of the most prized minerals for collectors.*

▼ *Phosgenite is a lead mineral that is rare enough in deposits to interest collectors. It becomes yellow under fluorescence.*

▼ *Heulandite, a white mineral with a pearly luster, much valued by collectors for its elongate crystals.*

▲ *Unlike hedenbergite, diopside contains magnesium in place of iron, which brightens up its crystal. This one can be cut as a gem.*

▼ *When transparent, benitoite can be faceted. A crystal of gem quality larger than 2 carats (0.4 g [0.14 oz.]) exceeds a sapphire in value.*

▲ *Hedenbergite. This calcium and iron silicate similar to diopside is much less common than diopside, and therefore is highly prized in collections.*

▼ *Bournonite with white quartz. Very sought after by collectors because of its characteristic twinning, called "cogwheel ore" by miners.*

Soft Brazilianite

Brazilianite was discovered in Brazil in 1945. Its clear yellow-green crystals were at first mistaken for chrysoberyl, but it was quickly revealed to be unsuitable as a gem because it lacks the hardness of chrysoberyl. It has since become a highly valued collectors' mineral.

◀ *Collected for its blade-like crystals, descloizite also is of economic interest, because it is rich in uranium.*

▶ *Discovered at the same time as benitoite in the deposit in San Benito, California, neptunite is an equally rare stone, greatly prized for the quality of its crystals.*

◀ *Benitoite in white natrolite. San Benito County, California, is the only deposit in the world of this rare stone, discovered in 1907.*

▶ *Danburite. Its transparent yellow variety, which is suitable for cutting, is highly valued. This variety is mostly mined in Mogok, Burma, with precious rubies.*

Unusual Minerals

Meteorites

▲ *Olivine that is present in our soil (shown here in a volcanic bomb) is also found in meteorites; some can even be faceted.*

▼ *Moldavites. Green moldavite is a gem variety of tectite that is collected in Bohemia and Moldavia, more than 300 km (186 mi.) from the place where the meteorite hit.*

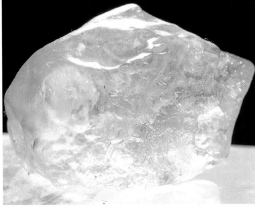

▲ *Tectite from Libya. A yellow variety of tectite is found in Libya that is rarer than moldavite and can be cut as a gemstone.*

▼ *Tectites are fragments of terrestrial rocks that have literally melted upon impact with a meteorite; they are transformed into silica glass.*

A 12-kg (26-lb.) meteorite hit the hood of a car at a speed of 54,000 km/hour (33,500 mi./hr.) in New York State on October 9, 1992; however, it created more fear than harm, as the driver had left the car to do her errands. Each year, 20,000 tons of this material comes to us from space, at a speed 4,000 times faster than a cannonball. There's no reason to panic, because the vast majority is "cosmic dust," micrometeorites smaller than a millimeter. They are completely harmless, unless one hits you in the eye. About 100 meteorites exceeding 100 kg (220 lbs.) are statistically capable of reaching the earth each year. Because the earth is two-thirds ocean, most of the stones sink into the water. The probability of a bolide 10 km (6.2 mi.) in diameter suddenly falling on our planet someday is one in 100 million years. It would have an impact 500 million times greater than the bomb dropped on Hiroshima in 1945. Unlikely? It is believed that an object of this magnitude struck the earth 65 million years ago, causing unprecedented geologic upheaval (the Cretaceous-Tertiary boundary) and the disappearance of the dinosaurs. The impact of this meteor is thought to be the crater of Chicxulub, in Mexico, 200 km (124 mi.) long.

In order to reach us, meteorites have traveled for millions of years. They come from a specific place in interstellar called the "asteroid belt," which revolves between Mars and Jupiter, and which may well contain pieces of an exploded planet. As old as the earth—4.55 million years—meteorites are made of a much purer material than the earth, similar to what the earth must have been like when it was formed. Each object that falls to earth provides an opportunity for scientists to go back a little farther in investigating the mystery of our origin.

▼ *Tectite from Thailand. The force of the impact causes the tectites to become vitrified, like obsidian, which is of volcanic origin.*

◀ *Meteorite that fell in Croatia on May 26, 1751. The speed of the meteorite's fall was 15 km/s (9.3 mi./sec.), 4,000 times the speed of a cannonball, of the time.*

▼ *Tectite from the Ivory Coast. They come from the meteorite crater of Bosumtwi, more than 200 km (124 mi.) from the deposit.*

HIRASCHINA (IID)

◀ *The meteoritic origin of tectites was not unanimously agreed to by the world's scientists, although the tectites are always found in the area of craters.*

◀ The Ries crater in Nördlinger, Germany, 25 km (15.5 mi.) in diameter, is a meteorite impact crater that produced moldavites found 300 km (186 mi.) from there.

▶ Tectites are traditionally worn as amulets. Because of their origin, some people believe they bring ethereal spirits back to earth.

▼ Moldavite as a pendant. Moldavite is considered to be a stone that revitalizes one because it is strongly charged with cosmic energy.

Minerals from the Sky

There are three kinds of meteorites, based on their composition: siderites, or iron meteorites, with a high metal content (on left); aerolites, or stony meteorites, which are rich in silicates; and siderolites, meteorites that contain as many silicates as metals (most often, pyroxenes and olivine in an iron-nickel matrix).

▼ Meteorites that have fallen in Namibia. Although micrometeorites (smaller than 1 mm [0.04 in.]) are predominant, there are specimens up to 100 km (62 mi.) in diameter.

▲ Gibbeon meteorites. The meteorites have a thin black crust on the surface that has melted in contact with the atmosphere; however, the inside remains intact.

▼ Radioastronomy station in Nançay, France. The Nançay project includes the detection of possible extraterrestrial life in space.

◀ The observatory at Naçay, France, has powerful radiotelescopes capable of detecting the smallest interstellar body entering the atmosphere.

▼ The Observatory of Nançay, France. Unlike meteorites, meteors—or shooting stars—break up when entering the atmosphere; they do not reach earth.

▼ At Nançay, France, a flag has been designed to hail the arrival of extraterrestrials.

Landscape Rocks

▲ *Occurring principally in sandstones and limestones, landscapes like these above are also found in siliceous rocks such as jasper.*

▶ *The famous marble landscapes of Tuscany, in Italy, are called "marble ruins" or "hut stones," according to their designs.*

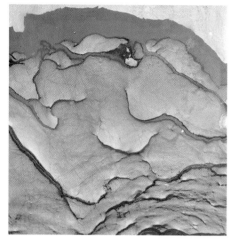

▲ *Landscapes are valuable; the rarest contain figures of people, and can cost up to $4,000.*

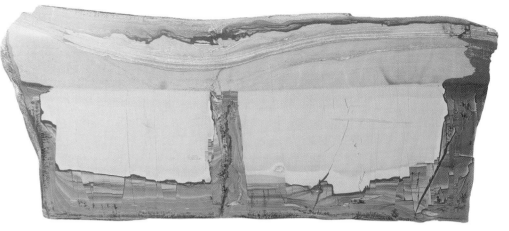

In the distance, tranquil huts rest in the soft light of dawn. A porcelain sky where a bird's flight is sketched with a fine black line. A Corot landscape? No, nature alone has presided over this masterpiece with marble as the canvas and iron and manganese as brushes. The Italians call these pictures "*pietre paesine*" ("landscape stones"), and the most remarkable come from the Carrara quarries in Tuscany. Since ancient times, marble from Carrara has been famous for its homogenous white, which has given it priority in statuary. Metallic oxides, iron or manganese, can be added to the material and design of these enchanting scenes. Often, the iron and manganese cause dendrites to be encrusted in the rock, also called "black bushes," or more complicated permeations bringing to mind ruins, called "marble ruins," or houses, called "hut stones."

Very much in demand as decoration, these landscape rocks keep their value (up to $4,000) only when nature has added elements like people, which is rare. Because it is rare, Renaissance painters loved to alter the landscapes, adding sheep and shepherds here and there to perfect their pastoral motif.

The Bristol marbles, in Great Britain, are also famous for their landscape fantasies, but any limestone rock can lend itself to this art; for example, because of the granular structure of the rock, sandstone with its coarser register may evoke the raw style of the great artist Cézanne.

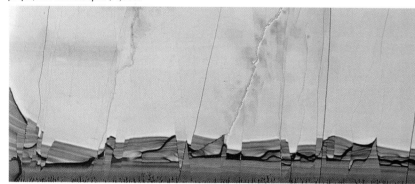

▲ *Seen in refined lines and bathed in the soft light of dawn, limestone landscapes seem to be produced by the palette of a watercolorist.*

▼ *The alchemists of the Middle Ages believed the landscapes had a supernatural origin, miniature reproductions of the great Creation.*

▲ *Marble landscapes must first be cut into slabs, then polished to make their designs appear.*

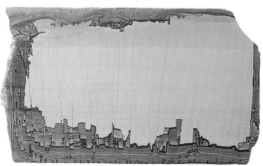

▲ *The most beautiful landscapes come from the marbles of Tuscany, where they are given the name* paesine.

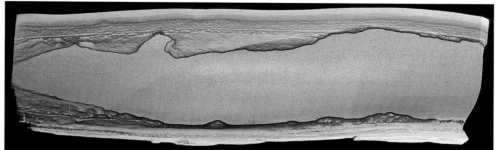

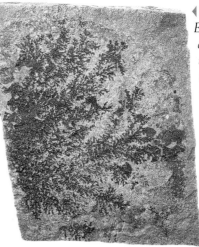

▲ *Sandstone with dendrites. Manganese oxide has drawn a plant motif in the rock, and here we see only the surface.*

▲ *Dendrites are the tree shapes caused by the crystallization of manganese or iron oxide in rock cracks (shown here, sandstone).*

◄ *Dendrite landscape. Encrusted into the rock, these dendrites are an irresistible reminder of a plant landscape, from which comes their name, "black bushes." Occasionally, dendrites are wrongly considered to be fossils, but don't be fooled by these pseudofossils. Like metallic oxides, native metals such as copper, silver, or gold can also make dendrites.*

The Agate Garden

The star, cloud, or moss patterns of agate have always struck the imagination. An old poem describes "tree agate" as a "a flower garden planted with bushes." This peculiarity caused it to be prescribed by alchemists for tree-cutters: worn on the belt, it was though to greatly increase one's strength and ease back pains.

▲ *Jack Cluff, an American artist, collects sandstone landscapes—and signs them.*
▼ *Brushed with great strokes, sandstone landscapes have the raw strength that Cézanne would envy.*

▲ *Sandstone landscape with designs in iron oxide. Red sandstones from Salamanca, Spain, are highly prized.*
▼ *Many of the sandstone landscapes available on the market come from the United States, such as this one.*

▲ *Sandstone, an ordinary rock made up of quartz and limestone, becomes more valuable when iron or manganese draw these fascinating designs.*
▶ *Tumbled stones of jasper landscape. Colored by bands and spots, this rock has its magnificent landscape effects.*

▲ *Linarite on galena. A "mossy" mineral colored blue by copper. Its name comes from Linares, in Spain, where it was discovered.*

▼ *Erythrite is called "cobalt flower" by miners. The cobalt in this erythrite causes the formation of the delicate rose color.*

Mineral Flowers

H ere, the pyromorphite needles form a carpet of moss over the rock; there, an encrustation of malachite has the pure effect of chlorophyll. Could the mineral world be related to the plant world by secret connections? No way! The mineral world is based on silicon chemistry; the plant world on carbon chemistry.

These strange shapes are due purely to the caprices of crystal growth. Vision can be fooled, but not touch. Mineral flowers are cold, hard to the touch, and often breakable. The illusion that they are plants is accomplished by the appearance of sand roses. A traveler crossing the Sahara Desert will think he or she is seeing a mirage when these sand roses spring up between the dunes, but it is only gypsum, whose growth has been frustrated by the sand grains contained in its crystals. Less inclined to think in terms of floral poetry, the Tuaregs, nomadic people in the Sahara, saw these sand roses as camel excrement that was petrified by the sandy winds.

The gypsum did not come out of the desert all by itself; originally it was dissolved in groundwater that evaporated as it rose to the surface, which caused the mineral to precipitate as a crystal, a phenomenon exactly like the process that creates rock salt from seawater (evaporites).

Sand roses are highly sought after as decorative objects; don't confuse them with barite, which also develops slightly less characteristic rose shapes.

◀ *The plant fantasies of pyromorphite are not just a joy for the eyes. This rock has always been an important lead mineral.*

▲ *As thin green needles, pyromorphite lays a plant carpet on the rock that is very lifelike.*

◀ *The radiating fibrous structure of minyulite looks like a carpet of seaweed on the rock.*

◀ *Libethenite. Rare in nature, this copper mineral is very prized by collectors because of its plant shapes.*

▶ *Okenite has fine white needles that make it look downy and fluffy like cotton.*

▶ *Aragonite on coral. This is a rare shape found in Mexico and the United States, called "iron flower" because it is found in iron mines.*

▼ *Taken from Greek, the name of pyromorphite means "in the shape of fire" because it was formerly believed that it was composed of molten lava. This mineral is famous for its fantastic plant shapes; it was held in high esteem by the alchemists of the Middle Ages, who extracted lead from it.*

▲ *The large tabular crystals of barite form rose shapes less frequently than gypsum.*

▶ *A gypsum rose in sand. Travelers who cross the Sahara may encounter this strange type of rose. Is it a mirage? No, it is gypsum.*

▼ *When siderite has a lenticular form, it looks like a carpet of dead leaves.*

▲ *The sand rose is gypsum, whose growth has been modified by the presence of sand grains in its crystal.*

▶ *A gypsum rose in sand. The Tuaregs from the Sahara thought "desert roses" were camel excrement mineralized by the sandy wind.*

▼ *Barite can also have rose shapes, highly valued by collectors.*

▲ *Geode with agate and quartz. Geodes are created by gas bubbles that are caught in magma at the time it begins to solidify.*

Geodes

It is a known fact that nature hates a void. When a hollow forms underground, it is soon filled up like an egg—a matter of a few million years where geodes are concerned. These curious mineral spheres are discovered by chance during production from veins; some can be 10 m (33 ft.) in diameter, others only a few millimeters. When they are opened, they reveal agate, amethyst, smoky quartz, celestite, smithsonite, azurite—all with the most beautiful craftsmanship and a rare clarity, a veritable treasure chest for collectors.

Geodes can form in a regular fissure or a solution cavity in sedimentary rock. When they form in volcanic rock, it is within the solid envelope of a gas bubble that is trapped when the magma begins to cool. These voids are quickly filled by mineral substances that are transported by water. This is how silica is introduced into a cavity to coat its walls and form a thick layer of agate. If agate doesn't take up all the space, other minerals also contribute to fill the void, for example, amethyst. Amethyst crystals are often large, because nothing is in the way to hamper their growth in the hollow of a geode. In Brazil, it is believed that geodes are good luck possessions for women who are about to give birth, no doubt because of their ovoid shape.

▲ *Blue smithsonite, a variety valued as an ornamental stone, sometimes coats the inside of geodes.*

▼ *The state of Rio Grande do Sul in Brazil has been famous for a century for the quality of its smoky quartz and its amethysts, many of which come from geodes.*

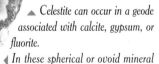

▲ *Celestite can occur in a geode associated with calcite, gypsum, or fluorite.*

◀ *In these spherical or ovoid mineral masses that are hollow in the center, two well-developed crystals have formed (shown here, amethyst).*

▶ *Quartz geode. The largest geode that exists today was found in Brazil; it weighs 35 tons.*

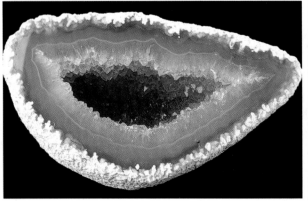

Azurite can occur as fine needles inside geodes. Here, a geode from Namibia in southern Africa has been cut into two parts.

Geode minerals formed in cavities (here, a celestine) can develop into large crystals because their growth is not restricted, as it often happens within rocks.

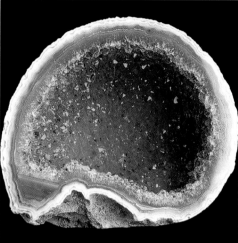

Quartz geode. This 20-kg (44-lb.) specimen is far from being the heaviest geode.

Quartz geode. Geodes can make up the theme of an original collection, although they are clearly more cumbersome than classic minerals.

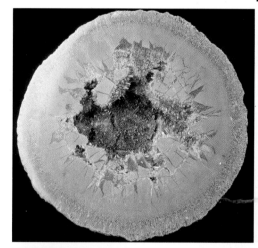

Septarian Nodules

Unlike geodes, septarian nodules are natural fissures that appear in the subsurface during the drying of large masses of clay. Minerals like quartz can occur inside them. Septarian nodules from the United States are famous for their perfectly transparent barite crystals.

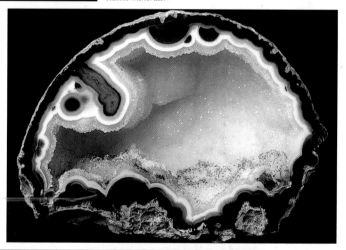

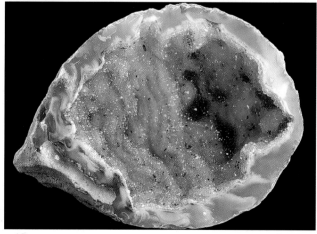

Here we see a diopside geode, from the Republic of the Congo. Diopside, especially the cat's-eye variety, can be cut as a gem when its transparency is perfect.

Crystals weighing several kilos (1 kg = 2.2 lbs.) are extracted from quartz geodes found in Brazil.

Uruguay, along with Brazil, produce the most beautiful geodes; these are mined in the Artigas region.

▼ *Exposed to X rays or ultraviolet rays, some minerals (shown here, hydrozincite) change their color. This is fluorescence.*

▲ *Hydrozincite is naturally white or yellow. When exposed to ultraviolet light, it produces luminous radiation that causes its color to change.*

Mineral Phenomena

Exposed to X rays or ultraviolet rays, minerals emit curious luminescent radiation that causes them to change color. When the rays are turned off, the appearance of the mineral returns to normal. This is fluorescence, so called because it was discovered in fluorite; its violet color under the effect of invisible radiation is a characteristic trait. This phenomenon is due to metals contained as impurities in the mineral, including manganese, cobalt, nickel, chromium, tungsten, or uranium, but never iron, which prevents fluorescence. Autunite thus changes from yellow to green because of the uranium it contains, and its fluorescence is an excellent way to detect deposits of it. Precious stones such as diamond, ruby, and emerald also have fluorescence because of the chromium they contain, but it does not have any effect on their value.

Fluorescence has wide applications in industry, as in the fabrication of light tubes (fluorescent lights); for example, the blue of neon signs is due to scheelite that is made fluorescent by tungsten. Greeks called yellow amber *êlektron*. In the sixth century B.C., they noticed that when rubbed with a cloth, amber had the property of attracting light objects to itself. They attributed this phenomenon to a particular "soul" that they believed was contained in the rock. It was electricity, whose energy was not harnessed until very much later, in 1800 A.D. in a Volta battery, during experiments with the properties of amber. The magnetic phenomena of minerals were also discovered in magnetite by the Greeks. The invention of the compass resulted from it, and also modern-day electronics; computer memories function largely on magnetic properties.

◀ *Brown chalcedony (blue by fluorescence). Some gems, such as diamond, ruby, or chalcedony, are fluorescent, which does not decrease their value.*

▼ *Brown chalcedony. If the luminescent emission continued when the energy source was turned off, it would be called phosphorescence (discovered in phosphorus).*

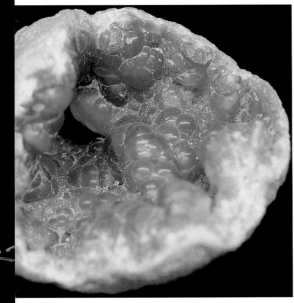

▼ *Green fluorite (violet by fluorescence). Fluorine was first described in fluorite, which gave its name to the phenomenon.*

▼ *Yellow autunite (green by fluorescence). The fluorescence of autunite, which is caused by uranium, is used in prospecting for this rock.*

◀ Halides (shown here, atacamite) make up a group of soft minerals that are mostly soluble in water, including rock salt.

▼ Although quartz is found as microscopic grains in sand, it can also develop into crystals weighing several tons.

▼ The Greeks called yellow amber êlektron. They noticed that when it was rubbed with a cloth, it attracted light objects; this was the discovery of static electricity.

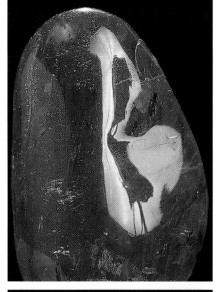

▲ Schorlite tourmaline, with albite and mica on orthoclase. Like amber, tourmaline produces static electricity.
▶ Giant quartz from Brazil. Giant among giants, a 70-ton quartz crystal was found in Kasakhstan in 1958.
▼ Platinum is the most dense of the minerals, 21.5 times heavier than water. Other minerals are so light they can float (seen here, pumice).

▲ Green fluorite. Heated to more than 50°C (122°F), fluorite emits light; this is called thermoluminescence, discovered in 1663.

◀ Rubellite tourmaline on quartz. The static electricity of tourmaline was formerly used to extract ashes from pipes. Dutch sailors were the first to use it, after they discovered it on the island of Ceylon in the eighteenth century.
▶ Known since ancient times for its ability to attract iron, magnetite was formerly considered to have magic powers. Spinel and pyrrhotite are also natural magnets.

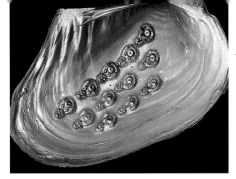

▲ *Deposits of mother of pearl on a shell. Mollusks naturally produce mother of pearl, a calcareous substance that covers the insides of their shells.*

▶ *Yellow amber (with a fossilized flower). This fossil resin, which was secreted by ancient conifers, is traditionally collected on the shores of the Baltic Sea.*

Organic Gems

Solid substances of both animal and mineral origin can be used in jewelry. Traditionally, they are put in the category of gems, the same as minerals. This is the case of the mother of pearl that coats the inside of shells of some mollusks. This is just finely crystallized aragonite (calcium carbonate). It has always been used in marquetry because of its iridescent reflections. Pearls are balls of mother of pearl secreted inside meleangrine oysters, conches, clams, or mussels. They are the product of a protective reaction of the mollusk to a foreign body encrusted in its tissue. To neutralize it, the mollusk coats it with fine concentric layers of mother of pearl, which after seven years of patient work results in a pearl.

Cultured pearls are obtained by grafting seeds of mother of pearl in oysters to cause this reaction. They are much less expensive than natural pearls, which can often equal precious stones in value. Consider the Lao-Tzu pearl, a 6.5-kg (14.3-lb.) specimen removed from a giant clam in 1934. It is valued at $34 million.

Red coral is the product of the calcareous skeleton of minuscule octocorallia that live in dense colonies at the bottom of warm seas. Like mother of pearl, it is a "biogenic" form—produced by a biologic process—of calcium carbonate, this time, calcite. Amber and jet are fossil products of old plants. They have been used for sculpture for at least 5,000 years. Shell comes from the carapaces (shells) of sea tortoises. Ivory, taken from the tusks of walruses, elephants, and hippopotamuses, is a mineral substance like our teeth or the mineral apatite found in rocks. Black ivory is taken from mammoths that are found frozen in the ice of Siberia; it is sometimes used for piano keys, but it is rare.

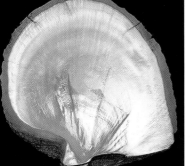

▲ *Pearl necklace with diamonds. Gems of organic origin are used in jewelry with mineral gems. Some, like pearls, can be prohibitively expensive.*

▲ *The word "nacre" (mother of pearl) comes from the Arabic naqqâra, indicating the very old tradition of its use in crafts in countries of the Middle East.*

▲ *Aragonite. Mother of pearl that is found in pearls and mollusk shells is nothing more than aragonite, a calcium carbonate. Dendritic aragonite is itself used as a decorative stone.*

▶ *Aragonite, or mother of pearl, can take on curious shapes. It is paradoxically called "coral." It is also called "iron flower" by miners.*

◀ *Engraved mother of pearl on a shell. Mother of pearl is considered very valuable in jewelry and in marquetry for its luster and its iridescent reflections.*

▲ *Pearl-producing freshwater mussels. Some mollusks, such as oysters or mussels, secrete valuable pearls, which are fine superimposed layers of mother of pearl.*

▶ *The Mediterranean countries use most of the coral they produce for crafts. Red is the most commonly used color, but white, blue, and black also exist.*

▼ *Yellow amber should not be confused with ambergris, which is taken from the stomach of the sperm whale and is used in making perfume.*

▶ *Blue aragonite. Aragonite is soluble in acid, just like the valuable pearl. A simple sprinkling of vinegar is enough to reduce it to nothing.*

▼ *Objects made of coral and shell. Coral is the calcareous skeleton of minuscule marine organisms, called octocorallia, which are related to the jellyfish.*

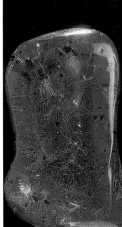

▶ *Calcite. Coral and marble have at least one thing in common— both are composed of calcite.*

▼ *A box of yellow amber from the Baltic Sea, from the seventeenth century. It belonged to the Queen of France, Anne of Austria. Amber from the Dominican Republic is also valuable.*

▲ *White calcite. Calcite, a calcium carbonate present in shells, is also a component of coral.*

▲ *Object made of tortoiseshell. Valuable tortoiseshell comes from the carapaces of sea tortoises.*

▲ *Synthetic star sapphire. Among other industrial applications, synthetic sapphires were used for a long time as needles for phonographic turntables.*

▶ *Fragment of an amethyst geode. The production of synthetic amethysts is not justifiable commercially, because the stone is abundant in nature.*

▲ *Synthetic ruby. Ruby is the first gem that chemist Marc Gaudin was able to produce synthetically in 1837, by reconstructing its formula.*

▲ ▼ *Amethyst has been obtained synthetically in the laboratory since the 1970s.*

Synthetic Minerals

Today, man is capable of replacing nature to create his own minerals—not imitations, but authentic minerals whose crystal structure and chemical composition are in every way similar to their natural models. The first synthesis was that of ruby, done in 1837 by the French chemist Marc Gaudin. He succeeded in melting (2,200°C [3,992°F]) aluminum oxide, to which he added chromium, according to the reconstructed formula of rubies. The synthesis of sapphire followed soon thereafter. Since then, both of these synthetic stones have found significant markets in electronics: the ruby for the manufacturing of lasers, and the sapphire for a long time as the needles for phonographic turntables. Synthetic emerald was obtained at the end of the 1930s by bathing beryllium oxide in an alkaline solution, all at 800°C (1,472°F). Seven months of growth are necessary to produce a beautiful clear crystal less than 1 cm (0.4 in.) long, which is less than what nature is capable of doing, although it takes nature several million years.

Synthetic diamonds were produced in the United States only in 1954, from a carbon base provided by graphite powder; today, a simple sugar will do it. Forty tons of these diamonds are produced each year. They are mostly used as abrasives in industry, because they have no transparency. It was not until 1970 that the first clear samples appeared that could be used as jewels, but their production has proven costly, less profitable than mining natural diamonds in the kimberlites of South Africa.

Hundreds of stones, from rutile to spinel, including lapis lazuli and opal, can now be produced synthetically. This doesn't include purely human inventions that simply don't exist in nature, such as fabulite, from strontium titanate, or YAG, whose name is made up of the initials of its components: yttrium, aluminum, and garnet, which have become respectable gems in the jewelry business.

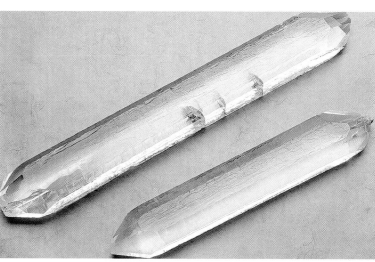

◀ *Synthetic hyaline quartz (rock crystal). Colorless quartz has been produced in the laboratory since 1905. Quartz is the mineral that has the most numerous industrial uses. Synthetic quartz is used today as a replacement for natural quartz in the production of watch oscillators, for the definition of emission frequencies of radio stations, and for the emission of ultrasound.*

◄ *Fire opal, like lapis lazuli, can be reproduced in the laboratory.*

▶ *Spinel (shown here, a raw natural crystal) is a gem that is in great demand for jewelry. Its name comes from the Latin spina ("spine"), which refers to its octahedral crystals with sharp edges. Rare in nature, today it is synthetically produced.*

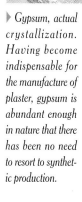

▶ *Gypsum, actual crystallization. Having become indispensable for the manufacture of plaster, gypsum is abundant enough in nature that there has been no need to resort to synthetic production.*

▼ *Colored quartz (shown here, smoky quartz) can be reproduced in the laboratory; however, its cost is clearly higher than the cost of natural stones.*

Test-tube Gem

Not found in nature, YAG was created in the laboratory in 1970 by combining yttrium, aluminum, and garnet. Its transparency and its luster have made it a good substitute for diamond, but much less costly than diamond, although its fire has a tendency to diminish once the stone has been immersed in water. Its commercial names of diamonair, diamite, and triamond are forbidden today in jewelry, because they can mislead the amateur about the value of the stones.

▶ *The laser used by the scientific police for fraud detection (shown here, a ring with a fake ruby) uses a synthetic ruby in its operation.*

▼ *Laser detection of a fake gem by the scientific police in Paris.*

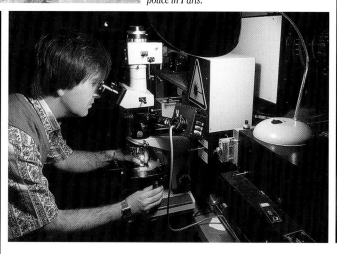

Stones That Grow

▲ *Can you grow a stone yourself? Nothing could be easier; in fact, the instructions are included in the box with the mineral "seed."*

▲▼ *Unlike a plant, a synthetic mineral needs to be watered only once—at the time the chemical solution is prepared.*

▶ *Do not leave "domestic" minerals within the reach of children because they are toxic.*

▼ *You need an average of two or three weeks to make your mineral "grow."*

Today, man is capable of accomplishing in several weeks what nature has taken millions or even billions of years to produce. This is the case with hyaline quartz (rock crystal), which has been manufactured only since 1905. This oxide of silica is the most common mineral on earth after feldspar, but it is only through synthesis that it is possible to obtain the purest and the best-formed crystals there are, which are prisms with six faces with pyramidal ends, and perfectly colorless. Its formation by synthesis has enabled scientists to prevent failures that always occur in nature because of impure crystals.

Translucent quartz fails either because of the presence of foreign material in its crystal or because it is unfortunately twinned. The recipe is simple: Seeds of silicon dioxide are put into an aqueous alkaline solution, which will favor crystallization molecule by molecule, something similar to building a brick wall. For this reason, the quartz has to be placed in

an autoclave, a hermetically sealed "boiler" that will reach a temperature of about 500°C (932°F) at a pressure 1,800 times that of earth's atmosphere. Inside, the crystal will grow at the rate of 2 mm (0.078 in.) per day—a speed much faster than in nature—but it must be perfectly motionless. The slightest oscillation will distort the ordering of molecules and this will open the way for deviations.

Today, the industrial production of synthetic quartz is several thousand tons per year. The cost remains high, meaning that this quartz will be used primarily in electronics or in the manufacture of clocks, as in today's famous quartz watches.

Since the 1970s, synthetic colored quartz, such as amethyst, citrine, and smoky quartz, has been produced, but it is too expensive to be used in jewelry.

▲ *Perfect crystallization on a simple thread—the effect of molecules that are slowly layered on top of each other slowly.*

▶ *This beautiful green mineral is a crystallized ammonia phosphate. It was obtained simply by "domestic" synthesis.*

▼ Silica seeds are first placed in an alkaline aqueous solution. The solution will favor the crystallization of quartz, molecule by molecule.

▲ The solution is placed in an autoclave, which is a "boiler" between 200 and 500°C (392 and 932°F), kept at a pressure of about 1,800 atmospheres.

▲ Annecy, France. There are various stages in the industrial manufacture of synthetic quartz. Here, it will be used in manufacturing watches.

▶ Inside the autoclave, the quartz must be absolutely motionless; otherwise, it is possible for the layering of the crystals to be distorted, and in the end, the crystal will be less perfect.

▶ The crystalline growth of synthetic quartz is 2 mm (0.078 in.) per day, which is a much faster growth than occurs in nature.

▲ Synthetic quartz, which has been produced since 1905, allows for the growth of much purer, better-formed crystals than those produced in nature.
▶ The industrial production of synthetic quartz is several thousand tons per year.

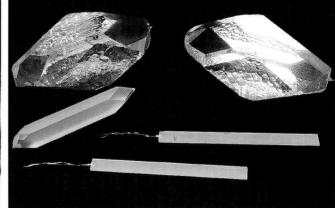

▲ Shown here are the stages of growth, from the seed to the final crystal, which is a prism with six faces and fine workmanship.
◀ The continued high price of synthetic quartz means that it will be used only in electronics and clock making.

GEOLOGIC TIME

ERA	PERIOD	EPOCH	YEARS (millions of years)
CENOZOIC (TERTIARY AND QUATERNARY)	QUATERNARY	HOLOCENE	
		PLEISTOCENE	−2
	NEOGENE	PLIOCENE	
		MIOCENE	−23
	PALEOGENE	OLIGOCENE	
		EOCENE	
		PALEOCENE	−65
MESOZOIC (SECONDARY)	CRETACEOUS	UPPER	
		LOWER	−135
	JURASSIC	UPPER (MALM)	
		MIDDLE (DOGGER)	
		LOWER (LIAS)	−200
	TRIASSIC	UPPER	
		MIDDLE	
		LOWER	−235
PALEOZOIC (PRIMARY)	PERMIAN	UPPER	
		LOWER	−290
	CARBONIFEROUS	UPPER	
		LOWER	−340
	DEVONIAN	UPPER	
		MIDDLE	
		LOWER	−400
	SILURIAN	PRIDOLI	
		LUDLOW	
		WENLOCK	
		LLANDOVERY	−440
	ORDOVICIAN	ASHGILL	
		CARADOC	
		LLANDEILO	
		LLANVIRN	
		ARÉNIG	
		TRÉMADOC	−500
	CAMBRIAN	UPPER	
		MIDDLE	
		LOWER	−570
PRECAMBRIAN	UPPER		
			−1000
	MIDDLE		
			−1600
	LOWER		
			−2500

AGGREGATE: Irregular grouping of minerals.

ALLOCHROMATIC: Color of a mineral due to the presence of a foreign body in its crystal.

CABOCHON: Gem shaped like a mound, but not cut.

CARAT: Unit of gem weight equivalent to 0.2 g (0.007 oz.). Not to be confused with a karat of gold, which is an indication of purity (24 karats for pure gold, 12 karats for an alloy of 50 percent gold.)

CARBONATE: A soft mineral, light colored, often transparent, formed by the contact of carbonic acid with a metal. Traditionally, the nitrates and borates are included in this group of 315 minerals.

CLEAVAGE: Property of a crystal to break regularly, forming fragments of an identical geometric shape (fragments of diamonds are always shaped with eight faces).

CRYSTAL: 1) Name of colorless quartz (rock crystal), and by extension; 2) geometric shape with flat facets that a mineral naturally assumes; 3) variety of glass made with lead oxide (lead crystal).

CUTTING: Putting facets on a gem crystal (about 100 minerals are suitable for cutting).

DENSITY (OR SPECIFIC GRAVITY): Weight of an object relative to the weight of an equal volume of water; a ruby, with a density of 4, is four times heavier than water.

DUCTILITY: Property of a metal; the ability to be drawn into a wire.

ELEMENT: Solid or gaseous substance, combined with others or not, to form matter; 110 elements have been categorized, three-fourths of them metals.

FACET: Each cut face of a gem (56 facets for the "brilliant" cut).

FIRE: Very brilliant sparkle of a stone, once cut; for instance, the fire of a diamond.

GEM: A mineral that can be cut and mounted in jewelry, or can be polished into a cabochon (about 1,000 minerals).

HABIT: Shape and appearance of a mineral, related to its crystal form.

HALIDE: Mineral composed of a metal and a halogen (chlorine, fluorine, bromine, iodine), producing chlorides, fluorides, bromides, and iodides, a group of 150 minerals, some soluble in water.

HARDNESS: Resistance of a mineral to scratching.

IDIOCHROMATIC: Color of a mineral that is characteristic of its chemical composition.

INCLUSION: Presence of a foreign body—solid, liquid, or gas—in a crystal, which often gives it color.

LAPIDARY: Gem cutter (from Latin *lapidis*, stone).

LUSTER: The reflection of light from the surface of the mineral.

MAGMATIC: Describing a rock that has crystallized from cooling magma, either at depth (plutonic rock) or on the surface (volcanic rock).

MALLEABILITY: The property of a metal that allows it to be flattened into sheets by hammering.

MESOZOIC: Geologic era extending from 200 million years ago until 65 million years ago.

METAL: Element characterized by its density, malleability, and ductility. There are about 20 that occur in the native state, and more than 50 that occur as metallic alloys.

METALLOID (OR SEMIMETAL): Describing an element with properties similar to metals, without their malleability or ductility (arsenic, antimony, bismuth).

METAMORPHIC: Describing a rock that has undergone a change in its form or nature (metamorphosis) as a result of pressure or heat.

MINERAL: A natural solid, either a single element or a chemical compound, that exists in an isolated state or occurs with other minerals in a rock in nature.

NATIVE ELEMENT: Element found underground in a macroscopic form, such as metal, metalloid, or nonmetal.

OPAQUE: Describing crystal that does not let light pass through it and is thus unsuitable for cutting.

ORE: Rock or mineral from which one or more elements can be extracted for a profit.

OXIDE: Mineral that is a combination of a metal with oxygen (or for hydroxides, with hydrogen and oxygen); a group of 520 minerals, including a number of gem minerals (corundum, opal).

PALEONTOLOGY: The science of the study of fossils.

PALEOZOIC: Geologic era extending from 650 million years ago until 200 million years ago.

PHOSPHATE: A soft, very colorful mineral formed by contact of phosphoric acid with a metal. The arsenates and vanadates are included in this group of 630 minerals.

PRECAMBRIAN: Geologic era extending from 4.55 billion years ago—formation of the earth—to 650 million years ago.

PSEUDOCHROMATIC: Describing the color of a mineral caused by light shining on the crystal, as the iridescence of opal.

QUATERNARY: Latest geologic era, which began 3.5 million years ago with the appearance of man (*Homo habilis*).

ROCK: Material that makes up the earth's crust; rocks are made up of one or more minerals.

SEDIMENTARY: Describing rock formed by the consolidation of sediments deposited at the bottom of seas, as in limestone, sandstone, clay.

SILICATE: Mineral composed of silica and oxygen; hard, colorful, often transparent. Many gems belong to this family, such as beryl, topaz, and garnet.

STREAK: Powdery trace obtained by scratching the mineral. The distinctive color of the streak is an excellent way of identifying a mineral.

SULFATE: A soft mineral, not very colorful, which is formed by the contact of sulfuric acid and a metal. This group includes the chromates, molybdates, tungstates, and tellurates: 315 minerals.

SULFIDE: Mineral formed by the combination of sulfur and metal. Included in this group are analagous compounds where the sulfur has been replaced by arsenic (arsenides), antimony (antimonides), selenium (selenides), tellurium (tellurides), or bismuth (bismides), a group of 540 minerals, including many important ores.

TENACITY: Resistance of a mineral to breaking.

TERTIARY: Geologic era extending from 65 million to 3.5 million years ago.

TRACE ELEMENT: Element found in a very small quantity in rocks, soils, or organisms, on the order of a milligram in organisms.

TRANSLUCENT: Refers to a semitransparent crystal that lets light pass through, but that a person can't see through. A translucent stone can still be cut.

TRANSPARENCY (OR CLARITY): Optical quality of a crystal that a person can see through; indispensable for a precious stone.

TWIN: Ordered association of two or more crystals, by proximity or interpenetration. Staurolite forms a twin in the shape of a cross.

Acknowledgments

The author and the photographer would like to thank Richard Eigenheer, mineralogist in Franconville,
for his unfailing availability and for the magnificent specimens that he placed at our disposal.
Thanks to Nazma Doobory for her valuable documentation.
Our thanks also go to the private collectors and to the museums of natural history;
without them, this book would not exist.

Photos

Front cover

From top to bottom and from left to right: agate, fluorite with quartz, emerald on calcite encrusted with pyrite,
mollusk fossil, fluorite, Venus hair quartz, mamellar rhodochrosite, malachite, citrine, fluorite with sphalerite.

Back cover

From top to bottom and from left to right: fern fossil, limestone landscape, dating of an antique ceramic
by heating, gold nugget, fine stones from Brazil, rubellite tourmaline, sapphire exploration in Sri Lanka,
Teide Peak, Island of Tenerife (Canary Islands), gypsum, echinoderm fossil.

Original title: *Les Mineraux et les Fossiles en 1000 Photos.*
© Copyright 1998 by Copyright Studio, Paris, France.
United States and Canada edition © Copyright 2000 by Barron's Educational Series, Inc.

All inquiries should be addressed to:
Barron's Educational Series, Inc.
250 Wireless Boulevard
Hauppauge, New York 11788
http://www.barronseduc.com

International Standard Book No. 0-7641-5218-1
Library of Congress Catalog Card No.: 99-72126

PRINTED IN SPAIN
9 8 7 6 5 4 3 2 1

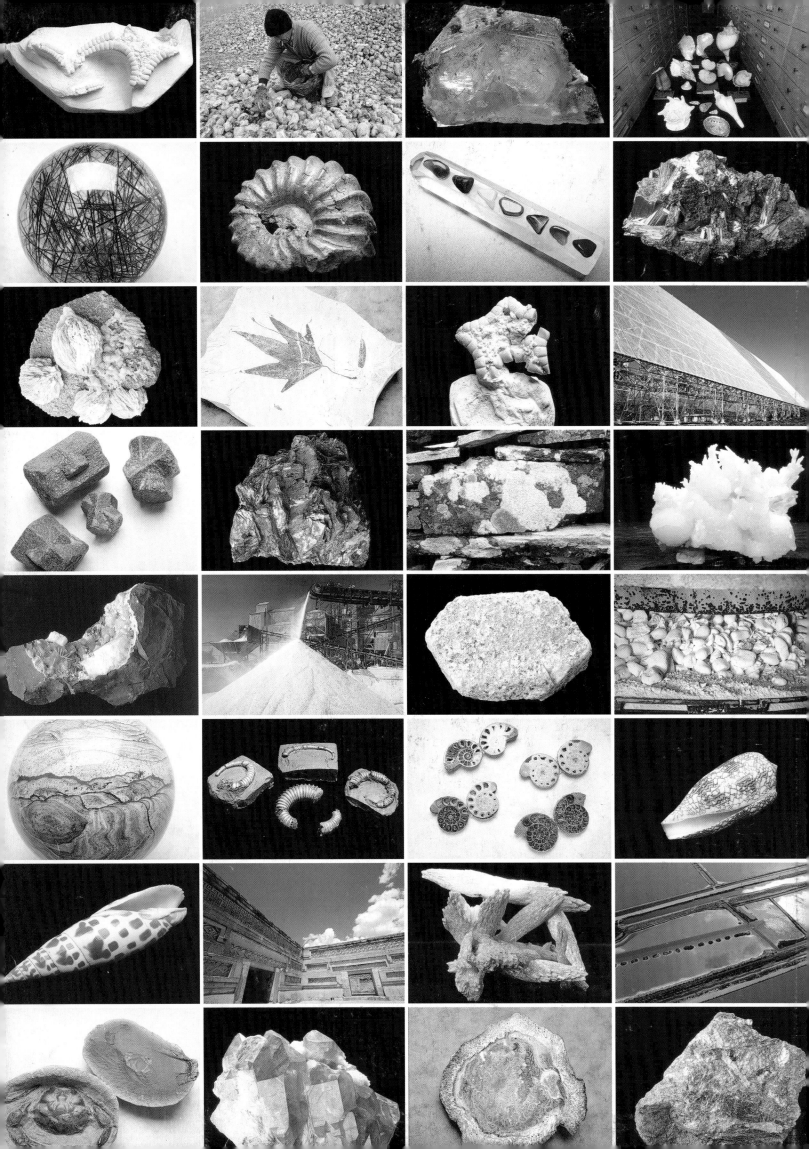